Learning through Story

Val Emblen & Helen Schmitz

Bright Ideas
FOR Early Years

Published by Scholastic Publications Ltd,
Villiers House, Clarendon Avenue,
Leamington Spa, Warwickshire
CV32 5PR
© 1991 Scholastic Publications
Reprinted 1992

Written by Val Emblen and Helen
Schmitz
Edited by Juliet Gladston
Sub-edited by Catherine Baker
Designed by Sue Limb
Illustrations by Jane Andrews
Photographs by John Twinning (page 5),
Bob Bray (pages 9 and 23), D. E. Lennon
(page 69), Anne Crabbe (page 79) and
Richard Butchins (page 85).

Cover designed by Sue Limb
Cover photograph by Martyn Chillmaid
Printed by Loxley Brothers, Sheffield
Typeset by Typesetters (Birmingham) Ltd

A catalogue record for this book is
available from the British Library.

ISBN 0-590-76437-3

Contents

Introduction

Stories, passed down through generations, tell of a people's history, their sense of values and their wonder at the world. For hundreds of years, families have told stories to each other. In fact we all enjoy sharing stories, whether they are tales of happiness, laughter, horror or sorrow.

At home, story times can be special times of the day, when adults and children can stop and share the experience of story-telling together. In nurseries and reception classes too, story time is often a pleasant shared occasion. You will often see children totally engrossed in a story, or joining in with repetitive phrases, because they are swept along by the power of the story.

The importance of stories

'The most enriching experience of all for many children is probably the open-ended exploratory talk that arises from the reading of stories . . . It also has a particularly important contribution to make to the children's imaginative development' (Meek, 1985, page 35).

When children are listening to stories they are not merely a passive audience but are actively involved. It is because they are actively engaged in the story-telling process that they learn so much from it. They review what they hear, reflect upon it, make judgements and, because of the 'multi-layeredness' of books, make many learning gains. Children can and do become totally involved in the world the story has created.

Through stories, children enter the realms of fantasy. They are able to explore the worlds and minds of others. They can play with ideas, emotions and feelings, extend their imagination and gain knowledge. They are not restricted to the here and now, but are free to explore ideas and concepts not present in their everyday lives.

According to Frank Smith (1978) and others (Meek and Mills, 1988), children are powerful meaning makers. Stories encourage them to take on new meanings regularly in a context of shared enjoyment. They learn about language and the different ways it is used. They learn new language forms from the written language of stories, which is different from everyday spoken language. Gradually, children take possession of the language of books, and they begin to learn many vital lessons about the reading process. From the moment they hear 'Once upon a time . . .', children should be able to join in the exploration of language uses. 'What texts teach is a process of discovery for readers' (Meek, 1987, page 19).

Stories and the National Curriculum

Children in the early years age group will be working towards the National Curriculum. However, identification of attainment targets and levels should not dominate the learning experiences of three- to six-year-olds. Teachers and parents should be clear in their own minds how the activities they provide lead to purposeful learning, although the ideas suggested in this book will encourage children to progress towards a higher level of attainment.

About this book

This book offers many ideas which are intended to extend and develop language and learning skills through stories. It also demonstrates that stories can be developed in a cross-curricular way. We talk about the active nature of stories – for example, how children become involved with story, how it can influence their play, their conversation, attitudes, concept development and so on. We ask, why does story time have to be at the end of the day? Why not read stories to begin the day, to stimulate the children's active minds?

We acknowledge the wide variety of previous experiences and skills which children bring with them on entering nursery or school, and therefore we have tried to include ideas to promote exploration, reflection and evaluation in children's response to fiction, no matter what their starting points.

Finally, we include a list of books which we have found to be both popular with children and valuable in stimulating a range of learning experiences. There is also a further reading list for teachers.

Choosing and organising books

Chapter one

At a time when there is a limited amount of money available to spend on books, yet hundreds of children's books are published each year, it is important that teachers, parents and carers make informed and careful choices when selecting books. We all need time to build up a stock of our own particular favourites, and the best way to do that is to *read* as many children's books as possible yourself. It is only by reading a wide selection of books that you can distinguish your favourite authors and illustrators, and can transmit your enthusiasm and enjoyment of the stories to the children.

Choosing books

By constantly updating and developing your own expertise, you can help the children to make their own informed choices of the books they wish to read for themselves. You will be able to 'match' certain books with certain children's interest levels, and generally show a greater understanding and knowledge of books that work with certain groups of children.

The way books are organised is an influential factor when encouraging children to choose books. So many children's books are wonderfully inviting and have exciting surprises when they are opened, so it is vital that they are displayed attractively and accessibly, to encourage children to browse and discover the world inside the cover.

Good books are essential to young children's learning, and therefore in this chapter we suggest certain criteria to consider when making your selection, and offer ideas about how to organise that selection.

Finding out about books

Ideally, the best way to find out about books is to spend time browsing in a good, well-stocked children's bookshop. However, not everyone is lucky enough to have a good children's bookshop within easy reach, so don't forget to use the local library which may also have a good collection. Spend time reading the books on your own, but also sometimes take a few children along with you. Their ideas will often direct you to thinking about young children's favourites.

Local teachers' centres may also offer a good selection of children's books, as will community bookshops where you will find books reflecting different communities, as well as multilingual texts and books written by local people.

Parents' magazines, journals and newspapers such as *The Times Educational Supplement* or those with children's supplements (*The Funday Times* and so on) regularly offer reviews of children's books. However, the best resource is always to read the books yourself. Publishers will often bring a selection of their books to your school if requested, and publishers' catalogues may provide brief descriptions of books and examples of the illustrations. There are also book clubs and other organisations which provide and supply books.

Where to find books

Bookshops
There are a number of well-known bookshop chains which are located throughout the country; Waterstone's bookshops in particular offer a guide to books which includes a children's section.

There are also a number of community bookshops, such as Headstart Books in Tottenham; New Beacon Books in Stroud Green Road, Finsbury Park; Sabarr Books in Brixton; Soma Books in Kennington; THAP Bookshop in Whitechapel Road (near the London Hospital) and the Walter Rodney Bookshop in Ealing.

Morley Books
Pegasus House,
116-120 Golden Lane,
London EC1.
These booksellers and bookbinders deal mainly with libraries, although they welcome enquiries from schools. They will reinforce both paperback and hardback books to extend their life in a busy classroom.

Book clubs
Many book clubs offer a range of children's fact and fiction at a discount.
• Books for Children,
Farndon Road,
Market Harborough,
Leicestershire LE16 9NR.
• Bookworm Club,
Heffer Booksellers,
20 Trinity Street,
Cambridge, CB2 3NG.
• Early Learning Centre,
Hawkesworth,
Swindon,
Wiltshire SN2 1TT.
• Humpty Dumpty Club,
Odhams Leisure Group,
Rushden,
Northants NN10 9RU.

• Jack and Jill Book Club,
Robinson's Children's Bookshop,
11 Bond Street,
Brighton,
East Sussex BN1 1JL.
• Junior Puffin Club,
Penguin Books Ltd,
Bath Road,
Harmondsworth,
Middlesex UB7 0DA.
• Letterbox Library,
8 Bradbury Street,
London N16 8JN.
• Red House Children's Book Club,
The Industrial Estate, Station Lane,
Witney,
Oxfordshire OX8 6YQ.
• Scholastic Book Clubs,
Scholastic Publications Ltd,
Westfield Road,
Southam,
Nr Leamington Spa,
Warwickshire CV33 0JH.
(In particular, their See-Saw club for younger children.)

Other organisations
• The Booksellers' Association of Great Britain and Ireland,
154 Buckingham Palace Road,
London SW1W 9TZ.
The association will give you advice on where to buy books in your area.
• The Children's Book Foundation,
Book Trust, Book House,
45 East Hill,
London SW18 2QZ.
They offer an extensive range of books, especially new publications, for perusal before buying. They also offer advice on organising book events and supply lists of authors and illustrators who will visit schools.
• The School Bookshop Association,
6 Brightfield Road,
London SE12 8QF.
They will give advice on how to set up and run a school bookshop.

● Centre for Language in Primary Education,
Webber Row,
London SW11.
They offer a variety of children's books and publications on language issues.

Magazines and journals

These journals cover the whole range of children's books, including those relevant to early years. However, always read the books yourself before reading them to the children.
● *Books for Keeps*
Available from the School Bookshop Association (see page 11).
● *Signal: Approaches to Children's Books* and *Signal Selection*,
Thimble Press, Lockwood,
Station Road,
South Woodchester,
Stroud,
Gloucestershire GL5 5ED.
● *The School Librarian*,
The School Library Association,
Liden Library,
Barrington Close,
Liden,
Swindon SN3 6HF.

What to look for

Books offered to children need to reflect the world in which we live and stimulate the imagination. No single book will be able to offer all the experiences children need, so it is important that children are given a wide range of reading materials, including both fact and fiction.

The following points can be used as a guide to selection. Provided with each category are some suggested titles of relevant books.

● Children need books which reflect the lives they and others in the community lead. Choose books which show positive images of ordinary families, including Black and Asian families, and families from other ethnic groups going about their daily lives. For example:
Wait and See by Tony Bradman and Eileen Browne (1988), Little Mammoth;
Ten, Nine, Eight by Molly Bang (1983), Picture Puffin.

● Choose books which include incidents and routines that children can recognise and identify with. For example:
Nandy's Bedtime by Errol Lloyd (1978), Bodley Head;
Five Minutes' Peace by Jill Murphy (1986), Walker Books;
You'll Soon Grow Into Them, Titch by Pat Hutchins (1983), Picture Puffin.

● Choose books to help children to understand that they live in a diverse society. For example:
Marcellus by Lorraine Simeon (1984), Akira Press Ltd;
Through My Window by Tony Bradman and Eileen Browne (1988), Little Mammoth.

● Choose books which show women and girls in a variety of active roles, making choices and decisions. For example:
Mrs Plug the Plumber by Alan Ahlberg and Joe Wright (1980), Young Puffin;
The Paper Bag Princess by Robert Munsch (1980), Hippo Books.

- Choose books which stretch children's imaginations. For example:
Time To Get Out of the Bath, Shirley by John Burningham (1985), Armada Picture Lions;
Meal One by Ivor Cutler (1980), Armada Picture Lions;
The Boy Who Was Followed Home by Margaret Mahy (1975), Little Mammoth.
- Select books to help children understand their own and others' feelings and emotions. For example:
Where the Wild Things Are by Maurice Sendak (1967), Picture Puffin;
Not Now, Bernard by David McKee (1980), Andersen Press;
Angry Arthur by Hiawyn Oram (1982), Andersen Press.
- Select lively, illustrated information books to support and extend children's knowledge. For example:
My First Nature Book by Angela Wilkes (1990), Dorling Kindersley;
My First Science Book by Angela Wilkes (1990), Dorling Kindersley;
The Very Hungry Caterpillar by Eric Carle (1971), Picture Puffin.
- Choose books which raise important issues for discussion. For example:
Janine and the New Baby by Iolette Thomas (1986), Little Mammoth;
Grandpa by John Burningham (1988), Cape;
Are we nearly there? by Louis Baum (1986), Magnet Books.
- Choose books which have simple straightforward texts. For example:
How Do I Put it On? by Shigeo Watanabe (1977), Picture Puffin;
Titch by Pat Hutchins (1972), Picture Puffin.
- Choose books which allow children to play with language and ideas. For example:
Each Peach Pear Plum by Allan and Janet Ahlberg (1978), Viking Kestrel/ Picture Puffin;
The Jolly Postman by Janet and Allan Ahlberg (1986), Heinemann;
Don't Forget the Bacon! by Pat Hutchins (1976), Picture Puffin.
- Children need texts which invite them to join in. Traditional stories such as 'The three billy goats gruff', 'The three bears' and 'The gingerbread man' are often the best. We also suggest:
The Great Big Enormous Turnip by Alexei Tolstoy and Helen Oxenbury (1988), Armada Picture Lions;
The Elephant and the Bad Baby by Elfrida Vipont and Raymond Briggs (1969), Picture Puffin.
- Choose books with pictures that tell the story. For example:
Rosie's Walk by Pat Hutchins (1968), Picture Puffin;
Sunshine by Jan Ormerod (1983), Picture Puffin;
Moonlight by Jan Ormerod (1983), Picture Puffin.
- Choose books with rhymes and poems. For example:
Mr Magnolia by Quentin Blake (1980), Armada Picture Lions;
Mig the Pig by Colin and Jacqui Hawkins (1984), Picture Puffin;
Peepo! by Janet and Allan Ahlberg (1983), Picture Puffin;
I Din Do Nuttin by John Agard (1983), Bodley Head.

- Choose funny books, joke books, pop-up books, books with flaps, books with holes for fingers and so on; all these help to make reading fun. For example:
Dear Zoo by Rod Campbell (1987), Picture Puffin;
My Presents by Rod Campbell (1988), Campbell Books;
Where's Spot? by Eric Hill (1980), Picture Puffin;
The Baby's Catalogue by Janet and Allan Ahlberg (1984), Picture Puffin;
Here's a Happy Elephant by Colin and Jacqui Hawkins (1987), Walker Books.
- Choose traditional, myth and folk tales from around the world. For example:
The Indian Story Book by Rani Singh (1988), Heinemann;
Rupa the Elephant by Mickey Patel (1974), National Book Trust, India;
A Thief in the Village and Other Stories by James Berry (1987), Hamish Hamilton.
- Choose multilingual books which reflect the languages spoken in your class. Many publishers have dual language texts, for example, Heinemann's *Spot* books (by Eric Hill). Various home language books are also available from the National Book Trust, India, and may be bought from Soma Books (38 Kennington Lane, London SE11 4LS).

Organising books

There are a number of ways in which you can organise the books in your classroom or nursery. You can have a central pool which everyone can use, or class books which remain in the class and are supplemented by visits to the local library. Having class books can prove restrictive because unless each class has a very good stock of books, the selection often becomes depleted and does not offer the range and variety needed. If you can share more books, for instance by rotating them with a colleague, then you will be better able to stimulate the children's interests.

Consider restricting the number of books on offer to approximately 20 in any one class. If there are too many books you may merely confuse the children. Leave the books in the classroom for about two weeks and try to read every single book to the children. They will be familiar with the content, and will want to 'read' the books for themselves. After a while, return about half of the books and take a group of children to the library to choose some more.

It is also important to:
- try to build up duplicates or even triplicates of the children's favourites in paperback;
- constantly refer to the books in your class, changing the displays often;
- display the books by showing the front cover, as the spines are not very interesting to little children;
- use shelving that is at a low level and easy for children to reach.

With all this in mind, set up your book corner (see page 15).

Making a book corner

Objective
To make an area in which children can spend time enjoying books in pleasant surroundings.

What you need
A good selection of books including those of the children and carers, book stands, screens, bookshelves in units or fixed to the walls at very low levels for the children to reach (see page 16).

What to do
Consider the area available. Even if you do not have a large area available for a book corner, much can be done to make a small area feel comfortable and self-contained. Try hanging paper streamers or mobiles from the ceiling. Use screens decorated with children's artwork or stories, or a row of plants to give a feeling of privacy.

Display the books so that they stand upright, making sure that they are attractively displayed and that each one can be seen easily. Use book stands to make a feature of one or two particular books, but do remember to change these displays regularly. Encourage the children to handle the books carefully, and to look after them well.

Favourite books should always be available for the children to share, and maybe these could be kept in a familiar place, for example in a basket.

Make sure that the book corner feels welcoming. Try to provide a rug and some cushions or bean-bags for the children to sit on, or even some small armchairs if possible. You could also include a selection of soft toys.

Leave aside one shelf for information and books for parents and carers to borrow. This encourages adults to spend time in the book corner and to look at books with the children.

Leave a felt board (see page 74) or a magnet board on a table. Make sure that the children have available different figures from stories so that they can retell the stories by themselves.

Follow-up
• Display books in other parts of the nursery or classroom, where they can become part of an activity. Try leaving some in the home corner.
• Select books with a theme and display these with relevant artefacts.

Boxes for shelves

Objective
To create more space for displaying books.

What you need
Boxes from supermarkets (preferably similar sized ones), wallpaper or coloured self-adhesive plastic, clear self-adhesive plastic, adhesive.

What to do
Either on your own or with a small group of children, collect some boxes from the local supermarket. Make sure that you select an appropriate box size to suit the books you want to display.

Carefully cover the boxes with the self-adhesive plastic or wallpaper. Remember to choose a covering that will enhance your book area, and which will blend in with the fabrics and colours. Finally, cover the boxes with clear self-adhesive plastic to ensure a longer life in a busy classroom.

You should then stick the boxes together to resemble a small shelving unit and use them for keeping and displaying books.

Follow-up
Collect offcuts of wallpaper to re-cover the boxes when necessary.

Making your own fabrics

Objective
To personalise the book corner by enabling children to make their own fabrics.

What you need
Plain light-coloured cotton fabric, wax crayons, thin paper, an iron for adult use.

What to do
Ask the children to draw patterns or pictures on thin paper. Make sure that they press hard and make a thick crayon mark. They should place the picture face down on the material, and then you can iron the back of the paper. The picture will transfer to the material.

There are various other methods of making designs on fabric:
● Using fabric crayons, the children can draw directly on to the fabric. If this method is used the fabric will be washable.
● Use tie-dye (see *Bright Ideas for Early Years, Art and Craft*, page 29).

Preserving books

Objective
To prolong the life of paperbacks and class-made books.

What you need
Clear self-adhesive plastic, adhesive tape, scissors.

What to do
It is well worth spending time at the beginning of term covering paperback books, and mending torn pages too! Ideally, you should regularly repair books and cover the books that you or the children have made. If children see you taking care of books yourself then it will encourage them to copy your behaviour. Talk to the children and encourage them to look after their books.

Follow-up
Ask one or two children to write notices for the book area, for instance: 'Please look after our books'.

The rabbits run for all they're worth, What is floating down to earth?

A wall story

Objective
To make a series of pictures to illustrate a story.

What you need
Paper, felt-tipped pens, paints, printing equipment, art materials.

What to do
Choose a story to illustrate. Use one that is not too complicated, but that is connected with a theme you are currently working on in the classroom.

Discuss with the children the illustrations you will use in order to display the story effectively through a series of pictures. Encourage the children to use a variety of art techniques, such as painting, printing, collage and so on. Do not draw the outlines for the children and let them fill them in, but encourage them to work for themselves. The illustrations do not have to be perfect copies of the originals!

17

When the illustrations are complete, write the text in neat and careful handwriting with a thick felt-tipped pen and display each section next to the relevant picture in the book area. Read the text to the children and encourage them to read it for themselves too. Leave at least three weeks before illustrating another story.

Keeping track of books

Objective

To set up a system of recording the borrowing of books.

What you need

A ticket holder for each book and for each child in the class, a large piece of card, small pieces of card, adhesive.

What to do

Setting up this system of record-keeping can be time-consuming, but once set up, it works very smoothly.

First of all you need to write out a ticket for each book that can be borrowed. All the ticket need have on it is the author and title of the book. It should be placed in a ticket holder and stuck inside the front cover.

Stick all the children's ticket holders on to a large piece of card and write each child's name on a ticket holder. Stick the chart on to the wall at child height so that the children are able to operate the system for themselves. When they borrow a book, the children should remove the card from inside the book and place it in their ticket holder. They may need help with this process to begin with but encourage them to be responsible for their own borrowing.

The whole process is then reversed when the books are returned.

Making a survey

Objectives
To provide the children with early experience of collecting and recording information, and to help them choose books.

What you need
Four popular stories, paper, pencils.

What to do
Fold four pieces of paper in half to make four small booklets. Stick a picture from a favourite story to the front of each.

The children should then ask each other to choose their favourite story, and you or the children should write their names inside the appropriate booklet.

Once all the children have made their choice they will be able to see which book is the most popular and which the least popular. Finally, display these booklets in the book corner.

An 'I like . . .' book

Objectives
To enable children to recall enjoyable stories and to help each other when selecting books.

What you need
A ready-made big book entitled 'I like . . .'.

What to do
This should be an ongoing activity which allows the children to recall an aspect of a book that they particularly enjoyed, or to recommend books to other children when and if they feel like it. Their recommendations may be in the form of pictures with you acting as scribe, or in the child's own writing.

Read the book to the children on different occasions to remind them of the range of books available. It can also be used as an informal record of the children's reading.

My favourite . . .

Objectives
To widen the children's knowledge of particular authors and illustrators and to help them to identify their favourites.

What you need
A collection of books by a specific author or illustrated by a specific artist.

What to do
Observe the children's reading and select a favourite author or illustrator, and focus on this author or illustrator for a week. Read her stories and display her books; it may even be possible to invite her to your nursery or class.

Encourage the children to talk about why they particularly like the work of this author or illustrator.

Follow-up
Choose another author or illustrator for another week.

Organising a listening corner

Objective
To create a quiet place where children can enjoy listening to stories.

What you need
A quiet, comfortable area of the classroom or nursery, a sturdy tape recorder (with headphones if possible), a selection of story tapes.

What to do
When compiling your selection of story tapes remember that as well as the commercially produced ones you can ask teachers, parents, carers, older children and all sorts of friends to read stories on to tapes. Try to use a wide variety of voices, both young and old, and a range of accents and languages.

Set up the listening corner, making sure that it is in a place where the listeners will not be disturbed, away from the door or through routes, and where those using the listening corner will not disturb children doing other activities.

Organise the tapes and store them so that the children can find their favourite stories easily. They should be stored at a low level, with a picture from the story shown on the tape box.

Make sure that the children can sit comfortably on chairs around a table, or on the floor with comfortable cushions and the tape recorder placed on a low table.

The whole area should be decorated with the children's own stories and pictures to personalise it and stimulate their interest in the area.

Show the children how to work the controls on the tape recorder. If very young children are going to be using the tape recorder, colour-code the play button green (for go) and the stop button red. Encourage them to use the listening corner unprompted and as often as possible, looking at books and using figures and flannel graphs to support their listening.

Follow-up

● Have a variety of tapes available, including stories, rhymes, poems, music, songs and everyday sounds.
● Make a tape of sounds from local areas such as a farm, a street or a building site.
● Ask the children to record their own stories on to tape.

Story-telling robot

Objective
To make a story-telling robot.

What you need
Two large boxes, cardboard tubes, egg boxes, tin foil, adhesive, other junk materials, a tape recorder and story tapes.

What to do
Help the children to make a large robot. The body and head can be made from the two large boxes and the cardboard tubes will make good arms. Egg boxes can be used for eyes and other junk materials can be used to decorate the robot. Encourage the children to add their own personal touches in painting or decorating the model, so that they feel personally involved.

Once the robot has been completed, put a tape recorder inside the body where the children can reach the controls. They will then be able to hear the robot tell them their favourite stories!

Follow-up

The children can make models which are appropriate to a particular story, for example, a giant for 'Jack and the beanstalk'.

Story packs

Objective

To enable children to follow a story in a book by themselves.

What you need

A tape recorder, taped readings of stories, books of the same stories, plastic wallets.

What to do

Make your own story packs by putting a story tape, together with a copy of the book of the story, into a plastic wallet. The children will then be able to follow the text and look at the pictures in the book while listening to the story. Use a noise such as the sound of a bell or a spoon tapped against a glass to indicate to the children when they should turn to the next page. Put a set of four books into a pack so that groups of children can listen to a story together.

Make story packs with tapes and books of the same story but in different languages.

Follow-up

Put a table in the listening corner and set out on it various materials and objects which can be used to make a sound. The children can then experiment with sounds and textures while listening to stories.

Stories as starting points

Chapter two

There are many different types of stories, and children need to develop their knowledge and experience of all the different formats. This will help them to develop as authors themselves, and to learn to use story language. Familiarity with the form and language of story is a vital part of learning to read, which is in turn a vital tool for learning.

This chapter takes stories as the starting points for different activities. The first section provides activities relevant to six specific stories, the second section shows how children can use stories to devise their own games, and the final section provides story webs giving ideas based around five other books.

Books

Stories can be used to stimulate learning across the curriculum. The activities in this chapter are based around six books, and it will be necessary to read these books to the children in order to complete the activities successfully. However, it should be possible to use many of the ideas with other stories.

The Lighthouse Keeper's Lunch

Ronda and David Armitage (1977), Picture Puffin.

This story is about an industrious lighthouse keeper called Mr Grinling and his ingenious wife. It describes Mrs Grinling's efforts to prevent three scavenging seagulls from eating Mr Grinling's delicious lunches as they are winched across to the lighthouse. Her strategies include sending their cat, Hamish, in a basket alongside the food to frighten off the seagulls. However, poor Hamish does not enjoy the journey, and once again the seagulls snatch the food. Eventually Mrs Grinling thinks of a master plan to defeat the scavengers so that Mr Grinling can eat his lunch once again.

This book provides opportunities for working around themes of food and sea.

Why do we have lighthouses?

Objective

To find out what knowledge the children have about lighthouses; their functions, who lives in them and why.

What you need

The Lighthouse Keeper's Lunch by Ronda and David Armitage.

What to do

Before you read the story to the children, spend some time talking to them about lighthouses. Do they know what these are, and why we have them? Ask if any of the children have seen a lighthouse; if so, can they remember where?

Explain to them that lighthouses are built to warn and guide sailors and fishermen so that they avoid crashing their ships and boats into rocks or getting stuck on sandy beaches or running aground.

Follow-up

● Read *The Lighthouse Keeper's Lunch* to the children.

● Make a display based on the book. Cut out pictures of lighthouses such as Southwold, Beachy Head, Mull of Kintyre and Plymouth Hoe, and mount them by the display. Encourage the children to draw, paint or make models of lighthouses.

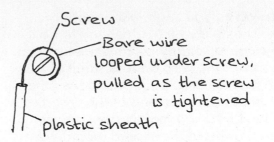

Make a lighthouse

Objective

To encourage the children to investigate electricity.

What you need

A torch bulb, a bulb holder, a battery, single-strand bell wire, a plastic salt carton or washing-up liquid bottle, a fish-paste jar, adhesive tape.

What to do

First make a simple electric circuit (see diagram). Don't use a battery which has a higher voltage than the bulb.

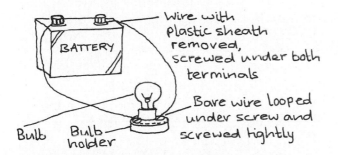

Remove the plastic sheath from the ends of the bell wire to make a connection. Loop the wire under the screws on the bulb holder so that the wire is pulled under the screws as they are tightened (see diagram).

Then fix your circuit through the salt carton (remembering to leave yourself enough wire for the purpose). Place the bulb holder at the top of the carton and cover it with the inverted paste jar (see diagram). Fix the jar in place with adhesive tape.

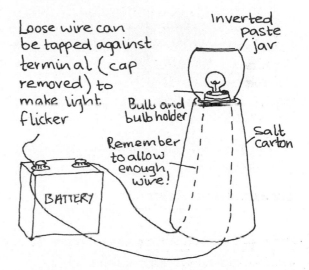

You can easily make the light flash by having one loose wire which is repeatedly tapped against the terminal of the battery, when the terminal cap has been removed see diagram).

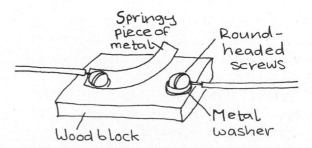

However, you might find it easier to make a simple switch. One way to do this is to screw a springy piece of metal over one end of the wire on to a small block of wood (see diagram). Attach the other wire at the opposite end of the wood so that the metal can make easy contact when depressed. Repeated tapping of the switch will make the bulb flash.

Young children have problems manipulating screws and screwdrivers, so they will need your help. However, the point of this activity is that the children will gain experience through handling the materials and attempting to make the circuit themselves, so it is important that you do not make the circuit without the children!

Follow-up
● Encourage the children to play with the model lighthouse.
● Let the children experiment with other ways of making lighthouses, perhaps using other junk materials.

Finding out more about making circuits

Objective
To encourage the children to investigate which materials conduct electricity and which do not.

What you need
Simple circuits, pieces of metal such as forks, spoons, keys and coins, plastic beakers, plastic and metal rulers.

What to do
In order to experiment with this activity, the children need to have had the experience of making a simple circuit (see the previous activity).

Some children will be interested to find out that there are different sorts of materials which can be used to bridge the gap left in the circuit and which will cause the bulb to flash.

Place the different metal and plastic objects with the circuits beside your lighthouse display so that the children are able to experiment with them.

After they have had time to experiment by themselves, ask a group of children to work with you. Experiment with the materials, discussing which materials will cause the bulb to flash, and which will not. Ask the children to think of any similarities in the materials that make the bulb flash. Introduce the words 'conductors' for the things that cause the bulb to flash, and 'insulators' for the things that do not.

Provide a further selection of materials (including metal and plastic) and ask the children if they can predict or guess which of these objects will make the bulb flash. You can record the children's findings on a chart for them if you like, showing their estimates next to the results.

Follow-up

There are many activities which can be based around an electric circuit. For example, try making a bell circuit for the classroom door or for the home corner.

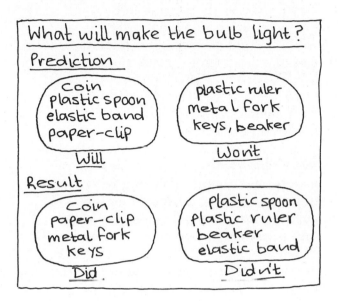

What will make the bulb light?

Prediction

Will
Coin
plastic spoon
elastic band
paper-clip

Won't
plastic ruler
metal fork
keys, beaker

Result

Did
Coin
paper-clip
metal fork
keys

Didn't
plastic spoon
plastic ruler
beaker
elastic band

A basket of food

Objectives

To encourage the children to plan ahead and recall events, and to help them develop manipulative skills in holding utensils, spreading and mixing.

What you need

Paper, pens, bread, butter, fillings for sandwiches, plain biscuits, icing sugar, beakers, fruit, herbs, fruit juices, natural food colouring, a large basket.

What to do

Ask a group of children to imagine that they are in the lighthouse, and ask them to invent some fun foods to eat. The food could all have a lighthouse theme, for example, 'iced sea-biscuits' or 'seaweed sandwiches'. The children could also invent special drinks, like 'froth on the rocks', 'seagull squirmer' or 'flashing fins'.

When you have finished discussing the food and drink with the children, ask them to draw their ideas on paper so that they have a plan of what they will make. When they have finished these plans, help them to make their drinks, sandwiches or special foods using an appropriate food colouring if necessary. What do the foods taste like? When the children have finished making the food they could display it in the basket. Talk to them about how they made the food and act as a scribe, writing down in sequence the recipe for each type of food or drink on a basket-shaped card which the children can decorate.

Follow-up

• Plan and develop the home corner to turn it into a 'lighthouse restaurant' (see page 32).
• Older children may like to make their own baskets as a problem-solving activity.

Seaweed Sandwich

Seagulls delight

Foamy freshener

Stop the scavengers!

Objective
To encourage the children to estimate and predict.

What you need
Scraps of material including open-weave fabric like muslin or gauze; small pots, soil, bird seed, grass seed, string, sticky tape.

What to do
Ask the children whether they can think of another way to help Mrs Grinling solve the problem of of the seagulls eating Mr Grinling's lunch. What other containers could she have used? For example, she could have used lunch boxes with lids, metal containers or other containers that have hard coverings.

Once the children have discussed the different types of containers available they should try the following experiment for themselves. Let them place a variety of seeds and bird food outside, either on the ground or in pots and containers. You should try to choose an area where the bird food is likely to be seen by the birds. The children should then cover the seed with different materials, for example gauze, muslin, metal, tissue paper and foil. They should also leave some seed uncovered. If they then number the containers or areas this will make recording easier.

Set up a bird watch; this can consist of two children at a time spending five minutes every hour watching what happens to the seed. Insist that the children stay very still while they watch, and give them a pad and a pen to jot down which covers the birds can peck through. To make recording easier you could make a simple matrix for the children, so that they can tick off which containers the birds go for.

Finally, record all the children's findings on a large wall chart.

Follow-up
Provide a display of books and pictures of common garden birds and introduce the names of these birds and their general characteristics.

Make a pulley

Objective
To give the children experience of transferring objects by means of a pulley.

What you need
A washing line, a pulley obtainable from a local hardware shop.

What to do
Together with the children, assemble the line and pulley system in your outside play area. For example, the line could stretch from a window to a piece of climbing apparatus or a playhouse. Exercise extreme caution, and ensure that the rope is high enough so that there is no danger of the children becoming entangled in it.

Try to make sure that the rope stretches to a piece of apparatus which you can pretend is a lighthouse. Relay baskets of food, real or pretend, from one end of the line to the 'lighthouse'. If you are restricted to working indoors try rigging a pulley system across the room. At least the children will still be able to see a working pulley system.

Once you have demonstrated and let the children play with the pulley, ask them to suggest other uses for a pulley system. Let them experiment with different uses and discover how well a pulley system works for a range of purposes.

Follow-up
Ask the children to make individual pulleys from cotton reels, some wood and nails. Hammer the nails through the cotton reels into the wood, so that you have two reels in one piece of wood and one reel in the other. Attach a long thin piece of wood between the two other pieces for added stability, and thread the string around the cotton reels as shown in the diagram. It is important that the children are allowed to make the pulley themselves, but reinforce the need for safety when using hammers and nails.

Give the children plenty of time to experiment with the pulley when they have made it.

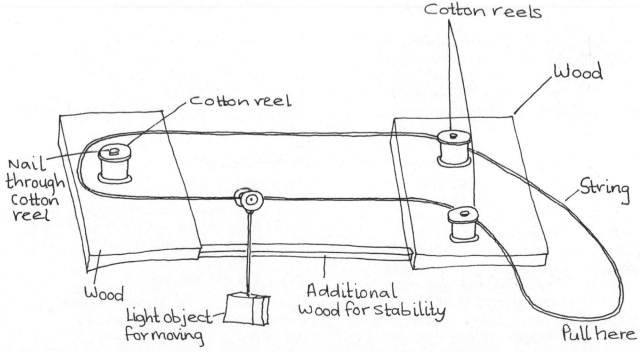

Cotton reels

Wood

Cotton reel

Nail through cotton reel

String

Wood

Light object for moving

Additional wood for stability

Pull here

Make a tasting table

Objective
To develop the children's sense of taste.

What you need
A variety of different things to taste, such as mustard, salt and mild chilli as well as sweeter tastes, strawberry jelly crystals, food colouring, teaspoons, small plastic containers.

What to do
Set up a 'tasting table' with a variety of foods placed in small, unbreakable containers. Make sure that you put only small amounts of each food in the containers and replenish them when necessary. Use foods that contrast, such as salt, sugar, cinnamon, nutmeg, mild mustard powder, ground cumin, ground coriander, honey, carob powder, grated onion, grated cheese and so on.

It is important to find out whether any of the children have food allergies, and to use natural foods as much as possible, avoiding foods with colourings, additives and preservatives.

Start off by reminding the children that the seagulls did not like the taste of the mustard sandwiches that Mrs Grinling made. Why do they think this was? You can then allow the children to taste the various foods. Once they have had a chance to experiment for themselves you should work with a group of children. Ask them to guesss the flavours of the different foods before they taste them. Introduce words like bitter, sour and sweet to help them describe the foods. Add some natural food colouring (green is a good one) to some strawberry jelly crystals. How much does the visual image alter the children's expectations of taste? For instance, green usually indicates lime, whereas red suggests strawberry.

Together, record the children's estimations on a large wall chart and then compare these with the actual flavours tasted. Record the real flavours on the chart as well.

Follow-up
Make a 'smelly' table, setting up different smells for the chidren to experience. For example, put some drops of strong smelling liquid, such as lavender essence, lemon and other citrus juices, vinegar and sandalwood oil, on small pieces of cotton wool, and place these in small containers.

What do you want for dinner today?

Objectives
To encourage the children to develop an understanding of a variety of foods and of the need to eat healthily.

What you need
Paper plates, adhesive paper, felt-tipped pens or crayons, food magazines, adhesive.

What to do

First of all, ask the children which foods they particularly like and to decide what they would most like to eat for lunch or tea. They could then either draw the foods or cut them out of magazines, and stick their meals on to paper plates.

Talk to the children about the types of foods that are healthy to eat, such as vegetables, rice, beans and salad; and what is not very good for us, such as too many sweets, cakes or chips. This time, encourage the children to think of a healthy meal and let them stick the appropriate pictures of food on a paper plate.

Follow-up

● You could display the plates together with plastic knives and forks, and discuss with the children the fact that not everybody eats with a knife and fork. For example, some people use their fingers, while others may use chopsticks.
● Make a pictogram or chart of the children's favourite foods.
● Choose some of the 'healthy' meals to make and share with the children.

Good enough to eat

Objectives

To encourage the children to make representational models and develop their manipulative skills.

What you need

Four cups of flour, two cups of salt, water, paint, varnish, oven.

What to do

Together with the children, mix the flour and salt with water, adding enough water to make a fairly stiff dough.

Working alongside the children, mould the dough into various food shapes, encouraging them to make the foods they like to eat. Ask the children to think of some food that Mr Grinling might make for his wife, Mrs Grinling. Make lots of foods that can be used for pretend play in the 'lighthouse restaurant' (see page 32).

Cook the dough in a low oven, about 100°C or gas mark 3, until it hardens.

Follow-up

Let the children paint their models, allowing them to mix the paints to match the colour of their food. Encourage them to think hard about the colours they are using rather than just giving them ready-mixed primary colours to paint with. When the paint is dry, cover the models with a layer of varnish to protect them.

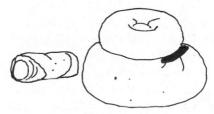

The lighthouse restaurant

Objective
To develop make-believe play around the theme of a story.

What you need
Card, felt-tipped pens, small pads of paper, ready-made dough 'foods', sets of cooking and eating implements, food magazines, adhesive.

What to do
With the children, turn the home corner into a lighthouse restaurant. To inspire them you could read the children some other stories based around food and eating such as *Mrs Wobble the Waitress* by Allan Ahlberg.

Help the children to decide upon a menu for their lighthouse restaurant. It should include some of the meals that they have already designed (see page 27). They must not forget to make a drinks menu as well.

You can then write out a number of menus on card, and the children can draw pictures of the different meals.

Encourage the children to cut out and make food collage pictures to decorate the walls and to tie-dye or print material for tablecloths and curtains. Try to link this in with the lighthouse theme, including nautical patterns such as sea shells.

Collect sets of plastic plates, knives, forks and spoons together with cooking implements from around the world. The children can then pretend to run the restaurant using the dough food which they made in the previous activity.

Follow-up
• Play with the children in the restaurant.

• Ask parents to come and cook real food which can then be eaten in the restaurant.
• Let the children prepare a simple meal, such as breakfast, for another class, choosing foods to suit most tastes. Let them write the invitations, lay the tables and so on.

The sand tray

Objective
To stimulate the children's creative and imaginary thought processes.

What you need
A sand tray, pebbles, cylinder bricks, empty washing-up liquid bottles and salt cartons, wooden or plastic boats.

What to do
After you have read *The Lighthouse Keeper's Lunch* to the children, make a feature of the sand tray. Turn it into a seashore and leave the bricks and empty cartons in it for the children to build a lighthouse at one end. Leave some small pebbles to be rocks, and little boats to simulate boats at sea. Let them also have a small tray of water so that they can pretend it is the sea. Spend some time playing with the children to stimulate their imagination.

Sunshine

Jan Ormerod (1983), Picture Puffin.
This story is told in pictures alone. The beautifully detailed drawings describe what happens when a young child wakes up rather too early one morning. The relaxed atmosphere suddenly changes with the realisation that the whole family could be late for school and work.

This is a delightful book to share with a small group of children. They love to pore over the pictures, telling the story in great detail, identifying with the little girl and her antics and giving her a special name.

Early bird

Objective

To encourage children to share personal experiences through group discussion.

What you need

No special requirements.

What to do

Before you share *Sunshine* with the children, ask them what they do if they wake up early. Share the ideas together. Some children might look at books, others might just lie in bed until they are told they can get up while others may watch the television or a video.

You can then look through the book, and once you have finished it the children can make another book called 'When I get up early in the morning'. This could either be a shared piece of writing for which you act as a scribe, or it could consist of the children's drawings together with your or the children's own writing.

Before school

Objective

To help children to understand the sequence of time, in particular the concept of 'before'.

What you need

Paper, felt-tipped pens.

What to do

Discuss with the children all the things they do before they come to school. Talk about getting up, getting dressed, having breakfast, having a wash, brushing teeth, journeying to school and so on.

Make individual books for the children so that they can record for themselves their morning routine. Let them draw pictures of each thing that they do. Then you or the children can write a caption for each picture. The text could be fairly repetitive, but it will be context-bound, which makes it easier reading for the children.

Follow-up

Put a photo together with the name of the child on the front cover of his or her book. The books can then be displayed in the book corner.

When I get up

Objective
To teach the children an action rhyme.

What you need
No special requirements.

What to do
First, tell the children the following rhyme while doing the actions.

When I get up in the morning,
I'll tell you what I do,
I wash my face [wash face],
splishety splash, splishety splash,
Then I brush my teeth [brush teeth],
scrubbity scrub, scrubbity scrub,
Then I brush my hair [brush hair],
And I put on my clothes [action]
And I runnity run all down the stairs [run
    on the spot].

Repeat the rhyme and the actions but this time let the children join in with you.

34

Follow-up
With the children, sing other songs and rhymes about getting up in the morning, such as 'Frère Jacques' and 'Down at the station early in the morning'.

How do you wake up?

Objective
To develop children's ability to collect and record data.

What you need
Felt-tipped pens, paper, large sheets of squared paper.

What to do
Spend time talking with a small group of children, sharing ideas about how you wake up in the morning. Do the children have an alarm clock, a radio alarm, a telephone call, or does somebody wake them? Does the dog barking wake them up or do they wake up automatically?

Suggest to the children that they ask their friends how they wake up in the morning. They should then list their findings and, with your help, record their data on a bar chart.

Get dressed quickly!

Objective

To help children to understand time; in particular, what can be achieved in one minute.

What you need

A selection of clothes from the dressing-up box including hats, jumpers, jackets and gloves; a minute sand-timer.

What to do

Ask a group of five or six children to sit in a circle. Place the clothes in small piles so that there is one in front of each child. Each pile should consist of a hat, scarf, jumper, jacket and trousers. Ask another child to be the time-keeper. His or her job is to watch the sand in the timer, telling the others when to 'go' and 'stop'.

As soon as the timer is upturned, the other children have to put on as many clothes as possible, until the sand has all run through the timer. They can then count how many clothes each has managed to put on in one minute.

You can reverse the process to see whether the children can remove the same number of clothes in one minute as they put on. Is it quicker to take off clothes or put them on?

Follow-up

Make a pictogram or a bar chart representing how many clothes the children managed to put on. Each child could draw herself and the individual items of clothing she put on and stick them to the chart.

How do you get to school?

Objectives

To encourage the children to work collaboratively and to represent their findings on a bar chart.

What you need

Paper, felt-tipped pens, coloured pencils.

What to do

In groups of no more than four or five, ask the children to talk about how they travel to school. Do they come by bus or car or do they walk?

In larger groups they should decide upon the categories they will need to display this information in the form of a bar chart. Ask the children to draw the categories and to stick them on to the horizontal axis of the chart. (The numbers of children will be on the vertical axis.) Cut out some small square pieces of paper and ask the children to draw themselves on these squares. They can then stick their pictures on the relevant place on the chart according to how they travel to school.

The children can ask other children and teachers in the school how they travel to school so that they get a broader picture. Very young children can record the initial information on a tape recorder.

Follow-up

In small groups, ask the children to ask each other 'true or false' questions about the chart. For example, 'Is it true or false that six people come to school by bus?'

How we travel to school

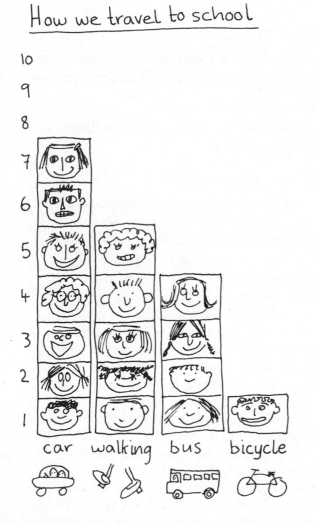

Tell the story

Objective

To support the fact that a story can be told with pictures.

What you need

Sunshine by Jan Ormerod, a tape recorder.

What to do

In a quiet area of the classroom let one or two children retell the story of *Sunshine* into a tape recorder. Together, write out or word process the story, allowing the child or children to illustrate it where necessary. It is important to allow the children to develop their own idea of the story wherever possible. You could retitle the story with the children's own names; for example, 'Hannah's book of Sunshine'.

Follow-up

Encourage the children to retell their stories to other children in the group.

What happened next?

Objective
To encourage prediction in children's own story-telling.

What you need
Sunshine by Jan Ormerod, a tape recorder.

What to do
Encourage the children to make up stories about what happened once the little girl in *Sunshine* left the house. Where was she going? Did anything happen to her on the way? If she arrived at school, was she late or on time? What happened when she reached her destination?

Tape the children's stories as they recount them, and then word process, type or write the stories from the tape. Put them all together in a large book so that the children can look at and read them together. Encourage the children to illustrate their own work.

Follow-up
Think of other stories that might have a similar theme. For example, what happened to Red Riding Hood when she went out? What happened when Goldilocks went for a walk and met the three bears . . .?

Make a map

Objective
To develop the children's observation and recall skills.

What you need
Large sheets of paper, felt-tipped pens, bricks, boxes, empty food cartons, adhesive, sticky tape, tissue paper, paint.

What to do
Ask the children to look about them very carefully as they travel to school or the nursery. They should look out for special landmarks, such as post boxes, telephone kiosks, roundabouts and local shops. Once at school you can take a group of children for a walk to the local park or adventure playground, looking all the time at the route you take.

On returning to school ask the children to either draw the route they have taken as a map on paper or make a three-dimensional model of the route. They might find it easier to make the model first and then draw the map from a 'bird's eye view' of the model. The models can be quite simple, using bricks to represent the shops or the park, or more complex models using empty food cartons and papier mâché.

Follow-up
Display the models in the classroom and use them together with the maps to broaden the children's knowledge of their local environment.

What do you eat for breakfast?

Objective
To develop children's ability to recall a particular item.

What you need
Paper, felt-tipped pens, a selection of different cereals, empty breakfast cereal packets.

What to do
Carry out a survey of what the children like and dislike for breakfast. Record these findings on a bar chart.

Encourage the children to think about related cereals, such as corn, wheat, oats and barley. They can then find out what is in their breakfast cereal packets. You should make a display of real cereals in the classroom, and perhaps even try grinding some wheat. Encourage the children to think about the sugar content of many of the breakfast cereals.

Follow-up
Display different cereals on a map of the world so that children can see where the different types of cereals are grown.

A river visit

Objective

To learn about and from the local environment.

What you need

Stale bread, paper, pencils, clipboards, plastic bags.

What to do

It is important that before you take the children on a river, canal or pond visit you plan it carefully. Before going with the children, make a visit yourself; this way you can ensure that all the necessary facilities, such as toilets and places to sit, are available.

Being near water can be hazardous, so make sure that each child is well supervised; ask parents to come with you, so that you have a ratio of one adult to no more than three children. You should prepare the children by talking to them about being safe near water; looking where they are going; not going too near the edge; taking care of their friends, and so on.

Also talk to the children about the sorts of things they might see on the visit, like ducks, boats and fish, and remind them that litter can be dangerous for wildlife.

Once all the preparation has been done you should be ready to go on the visit. Take some stale bread so that the children can feed the ducks. Point out things of interest and let the children sit and draw what they see, encouraging them to look carefully at the flowers and trees. They can collect any interesting objects they find, like stones, pieces of wood, feathers and even litter (if it is clean), but they should be discouraged from picking flowers.

Make a river display

Objective
To use the river outing as the basis for a display.

What you need
Objects collected by the children from the outing, pictures drawn beside the river, paper, adhesive.

What to do
Ask the children to sort through the collection of objects, looking at each one and trying to find any that go together. How will they lay out a display of these

objects? How can they make it attractive? Display the pictures that the children drew while on the outing alongside the collection of objects. When the display has been completed, let the children handle the things and discuss them. Why did they arrange them in the way that they did? Do they remember who collected which things?

Follow-up
● Borrow a goldfish for a few days and keep it in a tank near your display. Ask the chidren to watch it swim. How does it move? What does it eat? What do fish in a pond or river eat?
● Put stones and shells collected on the outing into the sand or water tray and let the children incorporate them into their play.

Floating and sinking

Objective
To investigate floating and sinking.

What you need
A water tray, a selection of objects, including wood, stone, plastic, cork, hollow things, things which are solid, a plastic cup, balls of Plasticine.

What to do
Gather a group of children around the water tray and examine the various objects. Let the children handle each object, and ask them to guess which will float and which sink. The children can then check whether they are right by putting the objects in the water. They should then sort the objects into two sets, one of things that float and one of things that sink.

Ask the children what they think will happen to a plastic cup. Will it float or sink? Let them test it in the water. In which set does it belong? They can also try putting flat objects in the water. What happens if they put them in with the flat side downwards? What happens if they put the objects in on their side? Ask them to put a ball of Plasticine into the water and then watch it sink. They should then hollow it out to make a boat shape. What happens when they put this in the water now?

Follow-up

• Provide a selection of boats for the children to play with in the water tray. Small boxes can be used effectively as boats, and you can make a sail by standing a triangular piece of cardboard upright in the boat, wedged with a small piece of Plasticine.
• How many plastic animals can the children put in a boat before it sinks? They can then try to guess how many animals it will take to sink boats of different sizes.

Wet and dry experiments

Objective
To investigate wet and dry.

What you need
Dolls' clothes, water tray, washing soap, clothes line, clothes pegs.

What to do
Remind the children of the part in *Mr Gumpy's Outing* in which the boat sank and all the characters fell into the water and got soaking wet and muddy.

Ask the children to wash the dolls' clothes and then hang them outside to dry. Make sure that the washing line has been set up so that the children can reach it easily. Talk to them about which clothes they think will dry quickly and which more slowly, and point out the differences in the material. If the children squeeze the water out of some of the clothes before hanging them up, will these dry quicker than those which are left to drip? Ask them to hang some of the clothes in the sun and some in the shade. Where do the children think is the best place for drying clothes? They should check the clothes regularly so that they can watch the drying process. Why do they think that some clothes dry quicker than others? What things help them to dry? Where does the water go?

Follow-up

• On a sunny day pour a small amount of water on to a hard surface in the garden or playground. Let the children watch as it dries. What do they think makes the water go away? Where does it go? How long do they think it will take to dry?

● Ask the children to paint pictures in the sun using plain water. They should use big brushes on a hard surface. They can then watch as their pictures disappear.

Acting the story

Objective
To use language to order the events in a story.

What you need
Large cardboard boxes or chalk.

What to do
Make a boat from cardboard boxes or draw an outline of a boat with chalk on the playground or classroom floor.

The children can then dramatise their own version of *Mr Gumpy's Outing*. Help them to recall the sequence of events by asking questions such as: Which animal got in the boat next? What did Mr Gumpy say? What did the calf do?

The children should get into the boat in turn as the story unfolds and pretend to be the animals, trampling or bleating or mucking about. When the story ends they must all pretend to fall in the water!

Follow-up
Show the children how to make zigzag books (see page 72). They should draw a sequence of pictures to retell the story of *Mr Gumpy's Outing* without using words.

A can and can't book

Objective
To help children to understand the reasons why some things are allowed and some are not.

What you need
Sheets of thin card or sugar paper, felt-tipped pens, crayons.

What to do
Work with a small group of children and remind them what Mr Gumpy said to the rabbit: 'Yes, but don't hop about'. Ask them to think of things that they are allowed to do in school or the nursery and things that they must not do when doing them. For example: 'Can I paint?'

'Yes, but don't make a mess.' 'Can I read a book?' 'Yes, but don't eat it.' The children will have lots of fun thinking of sillier and sillier ideas! Once they have thought up as many ideas as they can, the children can draw pictures of some of them. These should be stuck to two halves of a piece of folded card so that you have the 'Can I . . .' part on the left and the 'Yes, but don't . . .' on the right. These can be left in the reading corner once they have been completed so that other children can enjoy them.

Follow-up

The children can make riddle books by writing a description of one of the animals in the story on one half of the paper, for example, 'It is big and brown and goes moo'. Then on the other half they can draw a picture of the animal and hide it under a flap of paper. This way they can see whether their friends can guess the animal.

Poetry

Objective

To develop children's pleasure in selecting and using words well.

What you need

A large sheet of paper on an easel, a thick felt-tipped pen, a large sheet of card or a blank book, a selection of poems about water.

What to do

Read the children some poems or rhymes to do with water. Simple well-known ones are usually most effective with younger children, and it is always possible to adapt old favourites. Let the children splash their hands in the water tray as the poems are read and ask them to think of words which come into their minds as they do this.

You can then write all these words on the large piece of paper and turn them into a poem by adding the phrase 'Water is . . .'. For instance you may have 'Water is splashy. Water is shiny,' and so on.

These simple poems can then be written into a book or displayed as a wall poster, both of which can be decorated by the children.

Follow-up

● You can record a collection of water rhymes and poems on tapes which can be left in the listening corner.
● The children can paint water pictures by dampening thin paper before they paint on it. What difference does this make to their picture? These pictures can then be displayed with the water poems.

Modelling with dough

Objective
To see what happens to shapes when they are squashed and stretched.

What you need
Two cups of flour, one cup of salt, two cups of water, two tablespoons of cooking oil, a saucepan, a rolling pin, a kneading board.

What to do
Put all the ingredients in the saucepan and cook them gently for about three minutes, stirring all the time.

Allow the dough to cool and then sprinkle some flour on to a suitable surface for the children to knead on. The dough can be kept in a sealed plastic bag or container for up to a week.

. Ask the children to make characters from *Mr Gumpy's Outing* using the dough. They can use shaped cutters or cut round templates to get the right shapes. The children can then roll out their shapes, making them bigger and flatter. Encourage them to look for the differences, using words such as 'stretched', 'longer' and 'thinner' to describe the new shapes. Are they still the same animals when they are made flatter?

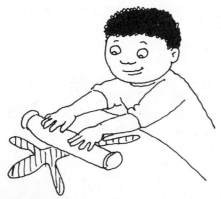

Follow-up
• Try the same activity with other malleable materials such as Plasticine and clay. What differences can the children find between these and dough?
• Ask the children to try mixing cornflour with water. Is it solid or liquid? Can they describe it?
• Record on a poster a range of 'dough words' such as soft, stretchy, squashy and squishy.

Sound effects

Objective
To experiment with making sounds.

What you need
Percussion instruments, including home-made ones such as dried peas in a tin, wooden bricks to bang together, a stick drawn along a LEGO block.

What to do
After listening to *Mr Gumpy's Outing*, ask the children to experiment with making sounds which represent incidents in the story; for example, the sound of the water in the river, the children squabbling, the calf trampling and the pig mucking about.

The children should supply their sound effects while someone reads the story again.

Follow-up
Ask the children to play a guessing game by doing each sound effect without the story being read. Can the other children recognise the incident each sound represents?

'Mr Gumpy had a boat'

Objective
To tell a story in another way.

What you need
No special requirements.

What to do
Most children know the song 'Old MacDonald had a farm' and so it is a good song to adapt. It may be a good idea, however, to let the children practise singing 'Old MacDonald had a farm' first, before altering the words. Once the children are sure of the tune they can sing the following:

Mr Gumpy had a boat,
Ee-i-ee-i-o,
And in that boat he had some children,
Ee-i-ee-i-o.
With a squabble squabble here and a
   squabble squabble there;
Here a squabble, there a squabble,
   everywhere a squabble squabble . . .

They can continue making up the verses for the rabbit, cat, dog and the rest of the animals.

Follow-up
● The children can accompany the song with untuned percussion instruments.
● Try to compile a collection of different animal songs and rhymes.

Rosie's Walk

Pat Hutchins (1968), Picture Puffin.

This book has become a modern classic. It tells the story of Rosie the hen, who goes for a walk and is unknowingly chased by a fox. The intriguing aspect of this book is that there are two stories told together, one through the text and the other through the pictures.

Woodwork

Objectives

To encourage proper use of tools and to develop manipulative skills.

What you need

Soft wood of various sizes, hammers, different sized nails, sandpaper blocks, a workbench or strong table.

What to do

When you have read *Rosie's Walk*, suggest that the children make the hen house, a cart or even a beehive.

Show the children how to hold the tools properly, and make sure there are enough adults to supervise the children who are using the tools, with usually no more than two or three working at the same time.

Follow-up

• Use the children's models to retell the story.

• Make models from other stories, such as 'The three little pigs'.

Using LOGO

Objective

To help children to learn to use LOGO.

What you need

Materials for junk modelling, a computer with the LOGO programme, a turtle.

What to do

Ask the children to make models of some of the things which Rosie walks past on her walk through the farmyard. Then place these models to represent the farmyard. If this is too time-consuming you could use building blocks or chairs to represent them instead.

Let the children walk around their model farmyard. Then ask one child to guide another round the course by just using the commands forward and backward, turn right and left.

Once the children have used these commands fairly successfully they can attempt to guide the turtle around the course, making better and better judgements about which movements they need to program into the computer.

Follow-up
• Place the farmyard objects so that the children have to make the turtle go round in a circle, square or triangle.
• Ask the children to create courses for each other to follow, using the turtle.

A three-dimensional map

Objective
To begin to develop the children's competence in simple map-making.

What you need
A table top, board or clear space, a model farm set.

What to do
Ask the children to use pieces from the model farm set to lay out Rosie's path around the farmyard. If this is done outside in the playground, the children can ride bikes or push carts around it.

Once the children are familiar with their model map of Rosie's walk they can draw it, and then try making a map of their classroom or nursery.

Shadow puppets

Objective
To teach the children about light and shade.

What you need
Black sugar paper or card, white pencils, lolly sticks or straws, sticky tape, a thin sheet of plain material, a bright lamp.

What to do
Ask the children to choose a character or an object from *Rosie's Walk*; for example, they might choose the windmill or the fox. Give them the white pencils and ask them to draw the character or object they have chosen on to the black paper. Help them to cut their drawings out and stick them to the lolly sticks or to three straws taped together.

Finally, hang the thin material in front of a strong light to make a screen. The children can then act out *Rosie's Walk* using their drawings as shadow puppets.

Follow-up
● Shine the light on the wall so that the children can make shadow puppets with their hands.
● On a sunny day, take the children outside to watch the shadows. Encourage them to make their own shadows move.
● Let the children make shadow puppets for other stories and use them on an overhead projector.

Follow-up
Let the children make up a sequence of movements for others to follow.

A farmyard walk

Objective
To give the children practical experience of the concepts of 'over', 'under', 'round' and 'through'.

What you need
Wooden building blocks, benches and mats used for PE.

What to do
Before the children arrive in the morning, you should lay out a series of obstacles in the hall, garden or playground, representing Rosie's walk around the farmyard.

Give the children some tasks related to the obstacles; for example, 'Go over three things and then stop', or 'Go round two things and then through one'.

A talking book

Objectives
To support children's early reading and to provide support for bilingual children.

What you need
Paper, card, felt-tipped pens, a large blank home-made book, a 'talking card' recorder.

What to do
Write and record the text of *Rosie's Walk* on separate blank 'language master' cards using a different card for each page of text.

Together with a small group of children, re-create the illustrations from *Rosie's Walk*. Stick these on the left hand pages of the blank home-made book and make pockets for the language master cards on the bottom of the right-

48

hand pages of the book so that they can be easily slipped in and out as the child reads and listens to the story.

Finally write the text in the book on the right-hand page, above the pocket. This encourages the children to 'match' the text and so keep the story in the correct sequence.

Follow-up
Make more 'talking books' and keep them in the listening area. Another suitable book is *Titch* by Pat Hutchins.

A three-dimensional picture

Objectives
To make a big picture and to explore textures.

What you need
Fairly thick card (for example, from a cornflakes packet), corrugated card, textured wallpaper scraps, string, adhesive.

What to do
Ask the children to make raised pictures to illustrate *Rosie's Walk* by sticking textured materials on to card. For example, the trunk of a tree could be made from corrugated card, and the leaves from raised patterned wallpaper. The children should then cover their picture with thin white paper and rub it with wax crayons. They can do this a number of times with different coloured crayons and experiment with using more than one colour.

Stick the rubbings on to a large sheet of paper to make the background of the picture and ask the children to paint big bright pictures of Rosie and the fox.

A big picture

Objective
To explore textures through printing.

What you need
Large sheets of paper, newspaper, small boxes, paints, a variety of things to print with, such as leaves, LEGO, sponges, cotton reels and pieces of Plasticine.

What to do
Ask the children to experiment with printing different textures and shapes. Then they should decide which things will be in the picture and which prints they will use to illustrate them.

They should print the background first, and then they can paint big figures of Rosie and the fox. Attach these to the picture with small boxes or pads of newspaper behind them to make them stand out from the background.

Peace at Last

Jill Murphy (1982), Macmillan.

This story is about a family of three bears. They all retire to bed, but Father Bear is unable to fall asleep because there are so many noises all around him keeping him awake. After roaming the house and garden in search of quiet, he eventually returns to his own bed and peace — only to be suddenly awoken by the shrill ring of the alarm clock.

Peace at Last is a wonderful story with which both adults and children identify strongly. Any parent with young children would recognise the desperation of lost sleep which is so brilliantly captured in this story.

I can't sleep

Objectives

To encourage the children to recall and relate past experiences.

What you need

No special requirements.

What to do

Before you read *Peace at Last*, ask the children what they do if they cannot sleep. They might:
- call for their parents to come and be with them;
- look at a book;
- sing songs;
- count sheep;
- ask to be cuddled;
- cuddle up to their favourite toy.

What other ideas do they have? Share with them some of the things you do when you have difficulty sleeping.

Follow-up

Read *Goodnight Owl!* by Pat Hutchins.

A collaborative picture

Objective

To encourage the children to work together.

What you need

Paints, pens, pencils, adhesive, large pieces of paper, fabric scraps.

What to do

Read *Peace at Last* together and look at the illustrations carefully. Choose one of them to form a display on the wall. An especially good one is the one on page 3 where the whole family is going upstairs to bed.

Ask one or two children to draw the characters for the picture. It is important to ask the children if they want to be involved. Help the children to decide how they should set about drawing their characters. Remind them to consider the relative sizing of the pictures as much as possible. Then ask two or three other children to either paint the bears or cover them with fabric. The bears should be cut out once they have been completed. Ask the rest of the children to draw and paint any other items they can see in the picture.

When you mount the pictures on the wall, build them up to make a three-dimensional effect by stuffing some newspaper behind the bear cut-outs.

Guess the sound

Objective
To develop the children's listening skills.

What you need
A tape recorder, tapes of everyday sounds.

What to do
Talk to the children about the many different sounds that are mentioned in *Peace at Last*. It helps if you can play a tape of these sounds recorded in your own home, such as the clock ticking, the fridge humming and the alarm clock ringing. After having read the story, play the tape to the children. How many sounds can they recognise?

Tape other sounds, such as cars, trains, running water, sirens and pneumatic drills. How many of these do the children recognise?

Leave the tape in the listening area so that the children can test one another.

Follow-up
Ask the children to make their own tapes of sounds in the school or in their homes.

Simple sound lotto

Objective
To encourage sound and picture matching.

What you need
Card, paper, felt-tipped pens, clear self-adhesive plastic, magazines.

What to do
Draw or cut out pictures from magazines which show things that make a noise. Lotto is a matching game, so you will have to use two copies of each picture. Some good themes to use are different forms of transport, animals, musical instruments and so on.

Stick nine pictures on each of five or six cards. Cover the cards with a self-adhesive plastic covering. Stick each of the duplicate pictures on to an individual small card and cover them with plastic.

Organise the children into groups of five or six and give each child a picture card. To play the game, you should shuffle the cards and then turn them over one at a time, making sure that all the children can see the upturned card. If the card matches a picture on a child's card then he must attempt to make the sound that the picture suggests. If the child makes the noise successfully then he wins it and can cover the matching picture on his board. The aim of the game is to cover all the pictures on your card, and during the game the children are not allowed to speak.

Once the children have learned how to play they can play by themselves.

Sound table

Objective
To give the children the opportunity to experiment with sound.

What you need
Objects that make a noise either by themselves or when hit with something.

What to do
Collect a variety of items that make different noises. You could have a selection of wooden instruments, wood blocks, a collection of metal things, and some plastic things. Let the children sort the objects into categories and experiment with the different sounds that they can make.

Introduce the children to bottle music. Show them how the different levels of liquid in the bottles produce different sounds. This should only be done under strict supervision.

Once the children have discovered different sounds let them play along to various nursery rhymes or perhaps provide the sound effects for *Peace at Last*.

Follow-up
● Make up a story with the children and provide the sound effects.
● Listen to *Peter and the Wolf* by Prokofiev. Point out the different sounds that represent each character.

Did you sleep well?

Objective
To introduce the children to the idea of nocturnal animals.

What you need
Pictures and information on nocturnal animals.

What to do
Talk to the children about nocturnal animals. Point out the nocturnal animals in *Peace at Last*, such as the bats and the hedgehog. Why do the children think that these animals stay awake at night?

Let the children find out about owls. Are any of them lucky enough to hear one at night? Talk about and look at pictures of different types of owl, and discuss where they might live.

Follow-up
● Take the children to visit a zoo where there are nocturnal animals.
● Read *Goodnight Owl!* by Pat Hutchins.

Who works at night?

Objective
To introduce the children to the fact that many people work at night.

What you need
Pictures of different people at work at night.

What to do
Find out if any of the children know somebody who works at night. When do these people sleep? Talk about the sorts of job done by people who work at night. They may be nurses, factory workers, people who sort out the first class mail on the 'mail train', policemen or women, and so on.

Follow-up
If possible, invite somebody who often works at night to come and talk to the children about his or her job.

A noisy book!

Objective
To enable the children to collaborate together to make a book.

What you need
Paper, felt-tipped pens of different thicknesses, adhesive, paper, card, scissors.

What to do
Explain to the children that you are about to make a *noisy* book together! It could be a book of animal sounds for very young children, or it may be an accumulation of pictures of various noisy things, such as a police car with a siren, an aeroplane, a road drill, and so on. For older children it would be exciting to develop a story-line.

Choose the theme, and either ask the children to cut pictures from magazines and catalogues, or encourage them to draw their own illustrations.

You can write any text the children wish to add to the pictures. If you choose an animal book, write the sound the animal makes. If the children are doing a story theme they can write their own sound captions, such as 'eek' or 'creak'. Try to choose captions that reflect the noise and encourage all the children to do as much writing as is possible.

Follow-up
Read the books together, making the sounds as you go along.

A restless night

Objective
To allow children the opportunity to recall and retell a personal experience.

What you need
A quiet and comfortable area.

What to do
Talk to the children about Father Bear in *Peace at Last* and how he woke up very soon after falling asleep. Ask the children if they have ever felt like that. Do they dream when they are asleep? Do they remember any of their dreams?

Relate some of your own experiences of not being able to sleep and tell the children one of your recent dreams.

Ask the children if they have any dreams or experiences they would like to share with everyone.

Follow-up
Read *The Land of Dreams* by Michael Foreman.

Oh no, I can't stand this!

Objective
To give the children experience of using a repeating phrase in the context of their own lives.

What you need
Paper, crayons, pencils, felt-tipped pens.

What to do

After you have read *Peace at Last* a few times the children will easily pick up the repetitive phrase (in fact, they will probably join in with you when you read the story!).

Talk with the children about the things that Father Bear could not stand, and why. Then discuss the things that the children can't stand. Try to keep it lighthearted rather than probing children's serious fears (which could be considered at another time).

Ask the children to choose one thing that they 'can't stand' and draw a picture to illustrate their feelings. Help the children to mount their pictures, and either you or the children can write a simple caption underneath, such as '"Oh no," said Jeremy, "I can't stand jelly babies!"' Try to encourage the children to choose different ideas.

Follow-up

Encourage the children to act out a very simple scene in pairs. During the scene they must say the phrase, 'Oh no, I can't stand this!'

How long do you sleep?

Objective

To develop the children's understanding and awareness of time.

What you need

Large and small pieces of paper, felt-tipped pens, pencils, adhesive, scissors.

What to do

Talk with the children about bedtimes and ask them if they know what time they go to bed. Do they know what time they wake up? You might need to speak to their parents about both these times.

Ask the children to draw pictures of themselves and to cut them out. Draw a large clock face, put in the numbers, and draw or make the hands. Fix the hands at one of the suggested 'bedtimes', say seven o'clock, and find out which children go to bed at this time. These children should then stick their pictures on the clock face, but not on the hands or on any of the numbers.

Encourage the children to write their names by their drawings. Label the clock, 'We go to bed at seven o'clock'.

Make similar clocks to show the other children's bedtimes and waking times. Older children could use the clock face to find out how many hours they sleep. For a different presentation, older children could also record their information on a bar chart.

Follow-up

• Make a display of clocks and parts of clocks, making sure that you use different ones, such as sand clocks, digital clocks and twenty-four hour clocks.
• Read *Clocks and More Clocks* by Pat Hutchins.

We go to bed at seven o'clock

Printing patterns

Objective

To give children a basic experience of tessellation.

What you need

Items from the nursery or classroom which can be used for printing, such as plastic cotton reels, DUPLO pieces, Unifix blocks, small wooden blocks, potatoes cut in half with a pattern cut into them; trays with ready-mixed paint spread on a thin sponge; large pieces of paper.

What to do

Let the children experiment with the materials, exploring the paints, the textures and the shape of the print. Then suggest that individual children try to print a line of shapes using one object only. Encourage them to move from left to right, starting at the top of the paper and working systematically in rows until they reach the bottom.

Very young children will need much more time simply printing, whereas older children should be encouraged to develop their printing skills further. Most children will find printing in rows quite daunting, but with encouragement, they will soon carefully cover the page.

Compare the children's printing with patchwork. Look at how the shapes fit together. Encourage the children to take more notice of shapes in their environment, for example tiles on the wall or floor.

Follow-up

Display the printing on the wall.

I remember . . .

Objective
To help children recall their own history.

What you need
No special requirements.

What to do
Tell the children a story from your childhood; for instance, 'I remember, when I was little, I locked my mum in the toilet because she threw my fairy slippers in the bin . . .'. Ask if any of the children would like to tell a story about when they were very little. Let them take turns to tell their stories to the whole group. Continue until you feel they have had enough.

Follow-up
Make two books, one of the children's own recollections, and another with their parents' memories. Word process the stories and stick them into the books, and let the children draw their own pictures by their stories.

My family tree

Objective
To give children experience of family history.

What you need
Photographs, felt-tipped pens, paper, adhesive photograph corners, your own family tree, simply made using photographs of your relations, but only going back two generations.

What to do
Ask the children what they know about their grandparents. Do they know how old they are? Some children might have great-grandparents; how many children know what that means? Tell the children about your grandparents and where and when they were born, and relate an anecdotal story about them.

Ask the children (and their parents) if they could bring individual photographs of their sisters, brothers, parents and grandparents to school.

Together with a small group of children, talk about their photographs. (Maybe someone has brought in a black and white photograph, which offers more opportunities for discussion!) Then, starting with the child's grandparents at the top of the piece of paper, mount the photographs carefully so that you won't damage them (it may be a good idea to use photograph corners). Below these photographs, mount the pictures of the child's parents, and finally, below the parents, mount photographs of the child and her sisters and brothers (if any).

Sam's family tree

Write the names of the children's relations (including surnames if possible) underneath each photograph, to show how and why names can change through generations. Finally, display the individual family trees around the classroom.

Follow-up

● Make 'family mobiles'. Ask the children to draw pictures of their immediate family, encouraging them to think of the front *and* the back of their bodies. Make holes in the tops of the figures and help the children to thread them through with cotton. Write the family name on a thin strip of card and thread the family on to this. Hang the mobiles in the classroom, next to the family trees.
● Read *Peepo!* by Janet and Allan Ahlberg, and discuss the pictures with small groups of children. Talk about the differences, as they see it, from their lives today.

What I did yesterday

Objective

To develop understanding of time past.

What you need

Paper, pens, adhesive, a ready-made book in which to stick the children's work.

What to do

It is useful to do this activity on a Monday when children can offer different ideas and experiences of what happened yesterday. However, do not restrict it to Mondays!

Talk with the children about what they think 'yesterday' means. Some children will have very clear ideas of yesterday, whereas others will remember something good that may have happened weeks ago. With very young children it helps to have a shared experience that you and the children can relate to and recall together.

With a small group of children, record their images of yesterday. You will need to scribe for the younger children, but encourage children to write for themselves as much as possible.

Once these recollections have all been written the children can stick their work in a book, decorate it and give it a title.

Follow-up

Sing songs with the children to reinforce the notion of yesterday. For example, sing 'Yesterday I went to play in the park, play in the park, . . .' and so on, to the tune of 'Here we go round the mulberry bush'.

Make a patchwork quilt

Objective

To help develop dexterity and hand-eye co-ordination.

What you need

Fabric, square templates, needles, thread, cotton, non-allergenic and fireproof stuffing, a piece of cotton material for the underside of the quilt, parents to help with sewing.

What to do

Ask the children to bring pieces of old fabric to school. Try to encourage them to bring a clean piece of their own old clothing to make it more personal. Tell the children that you are going to make a small quilt for the home corner, like the one in the story.

When you have collected enough different material, cut it into regular, even sized shapes using a template; squares are easier to begin with. Make this activity an ongoing one so that the children work together in twos or threes to sew their patches together. You will probably have to strengthen the children's sewing when the patches are completed; parental help will be useful for this.

Finally, sew the large piece of material to the underside of the quilt, leaving one end open for the stuffing. Place the stuffing inside and sew up the final edge. Maybe a parent could help with this too.

Follow-up

Make a display of patchwork, bringing in different shapes to use as templates and patches. Older children may like to try cutting their own shapes, maybe working with hexagonal ones.

Treasure trove

Objective

To share and value treasured items.

What you need

An area for display, treasured items brought in by the children.

What to do

Talk with the children about the importance of the patchwork quilt to Tanya's family in the story. Ask the children if they have something that is special to them, for example a teddy, a toy, a piece of cloth or a blanket.

Ask the children to bring their treasured item to school where they can have the opportunity to tell the other children about it and why it is so important to them. Let them have space to display their items, but remember that the treasures will probably have to go home with the children!

Follow-up

Make a display of a few treasured things. Encourage the children to take care of and value the objects.

Games from stories

Games can be based on almost any story. They provide a way for children to tell and retell stories they know, as well as giving them a variety of mathematical and language experiences.

Making a game

Objective

To reinforce a sequence of events, in particular the children's activities on their way to school.

What you need

A large piece of paper or card for the base of the game, felt-tipped pens, pencils, crayons, scissors, adhesive, die, counters.

What to do

Look together at a book such as *Sunshine*. Ask the children to think of and list the activities that they do before and on their way to school, such as getting up, brushing their teeth, washing and so on.

The children should draw each of the things they do and stick them in the order they do them around the board or in a snake shape, making sure that they maintain the sequential progression.

The children can play this game with a die, moving a counter along the board the same number of pictures as the number thrown.

For older children, you can write penalties or bonuses on cards which can be placed in the middle of the board. In this case you will need to add extra

spaces between the pictures, with the instruction to pick up a card. The cards should say things like 'Woke up late, miss a go', or 'Got up early, jump ahead three spaces'. The children should also be able to come up with good ideas for these cards.

Follow-up

The children can make their own games for other times of the day.

Track games

Objective

To help the children learn about turn-taking and about the language of games.

What you need

A sheet of card, felt-tipped pens, die, counters.

What to do

Make a simple track which represents, for example, Rosie's walk around the farmyard. Number each space in the track up to 20, 30 or 50 as appropriate.

The children can illustrate the game using incidents from the story. Then they can use a standard die to move their counters from the beginning to the end.

Follow-up

There are many variants of this basic game.
- The children can make up their own rules for moving.
- You can use a track numbered from one to ten and a counter which is red on one side and green on the other. The children should throw the counter and if it lands green side up it means they should move one space forward, while if it lands red side up it means they must stop where they are.
- Use a spinner numbered from one to four instead of a die.
- Use small cut-out figures from the story instead of counters.
- Add bonuses and penalties.
- Make a similar track and use it as a simple number line.

What's the time, Ms Fox?

Objective

To reinforce the concept of time.

What you need

A large space, a rectangle drawn on the ground to represent a hen house.

What to do

This is obviously based on the game 'What's the time, Mr Wolf?' but adapted to fit the characters in *Rosie's Walk*. For this game, one child should be chosen to be the fox. This child should then walk around in front of the other children who can all pretend to be Rosie the hen. They should follow the fox saying, 'What's the time, Ms Fox?' Each time the fox is asked this question she should turn around and say a different time, such as 'One o'clock', 'two o'clock' and so on. When the fox days 'Dinner time!' she must try to catch a hen before they can all reach the safety of the hen house. Whoever is caught by the fox must be the fox next time, and so the game continues.

Jigsaw games

Objective

To teach the children to match and recognise numbers.

What you need

A4 paper, card, thin black felt-tipped pens, die.

What to do

Ask a child to draw a picture of a character from a particular story on to A4 paper. Photocopy six copies of the character and let the children colour them. These pictures should be stuck on to card with adhesive and cut out. Each picture should then be cut into six parts. Ask the children to number the parts from one to six.

To play the game the children roll the die and take the part of the picture which matches the number thrown. If they already have the piece that corresponds to the number on the die then they can't take a piece. The winner is the first person to finish the jigsaw.

Follow-up

Ask the children to play the game with pictures of a number of different story characters, such as Goldilocks and the three bears.

Make a pack of cards

Objective

To help the children classify and sort objects.

What you need

Paper, thin black felt-tipped pens, access to a photocopier, card, adhesive.

What to do

Ask the children to draw the characters in a story, using only a black pen. Give the children a standard sized piece of paper and encourage them to draw the figures so that they are roughly the same size (this will not always work!). Photocopy a set of four of each character and mount all of them on to card to make playing cards.

The children can use the pack of cards to play card games such as snap, happy families and pairs, matching the same character each time.

Follow-up

● The children can colour their sets of pictures.
● Stick the photocopied figures on to card and stand them up in a menu holder or a piece of Plasticine so that they can be used as counters in a track game.

Making puzzles

Objective

To help the children with sorting and matching shapes.

What you need

Paper, card, felt-tipped pens, adhesive, scissors, plastic folders.

What to do

Ask the children to draw scenes from their favourite stories. You can then stick them on to card and, with the children's permission, cut the card into a number of pieces. Challenge the children to fit the pictures together again.

It is a good idea to store the puzzles in their own plastic folder so that the pieces don't get lost or jumbled. The children can keep them in their own bag or tray.

Follow-up

● The children can take the puzzles home to share with their families.
● A skilled parent may stick the pictures on to soft wood and cut them into shapes to make a more durable puzzle.
● Use the same pictures to make a bingo or domino game.

Story webs

The following story-based webs provide further ideas for activities based around specific stories. They are not intended to be exhaustive lists of detailed activities, but aim to provide basic themes on which your own activities can be based.

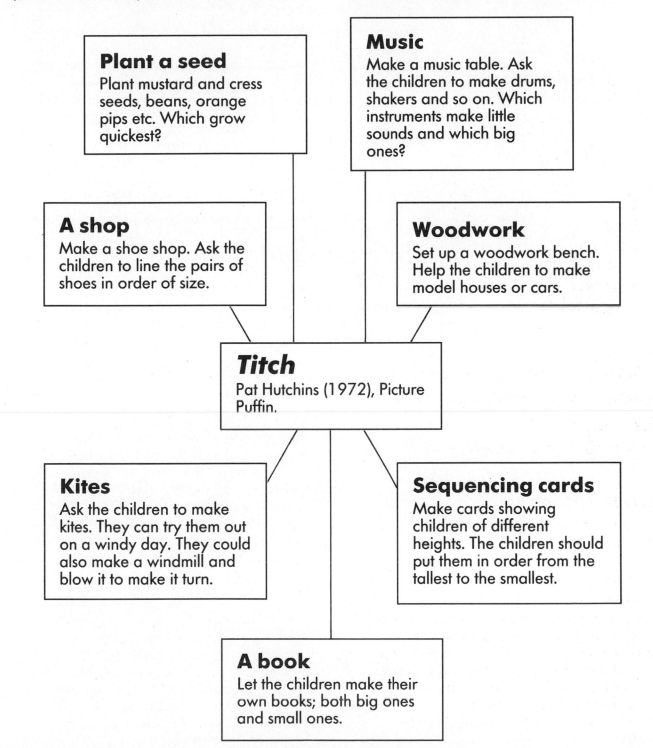

Plant a seed
Plant mustard and cress seeds, beans, orange pips etc. Which grow quickest?

Music
Make a music table. Ask the children to make drums, shakers and so on. Which instruments make little sounds and which big ones?

A shop
Make a shoe shop. Ask the children to line the pairs of shoes in order of size.

Woodwork
Set up a woodwork bench. Help the children to make model houses or cars.

Titch
Pat Hutchins (1972), Picture Puffin.

Kites
Ask the children to make kites. They can try them out on a windy day. They could also make a windmill and blow it to make it turn.

Sequencing cards
Make cards showing children of different heights. The children should put them in order from the tallest to the smallest.

A book
Let the children make their own books; both big ones and small ones.

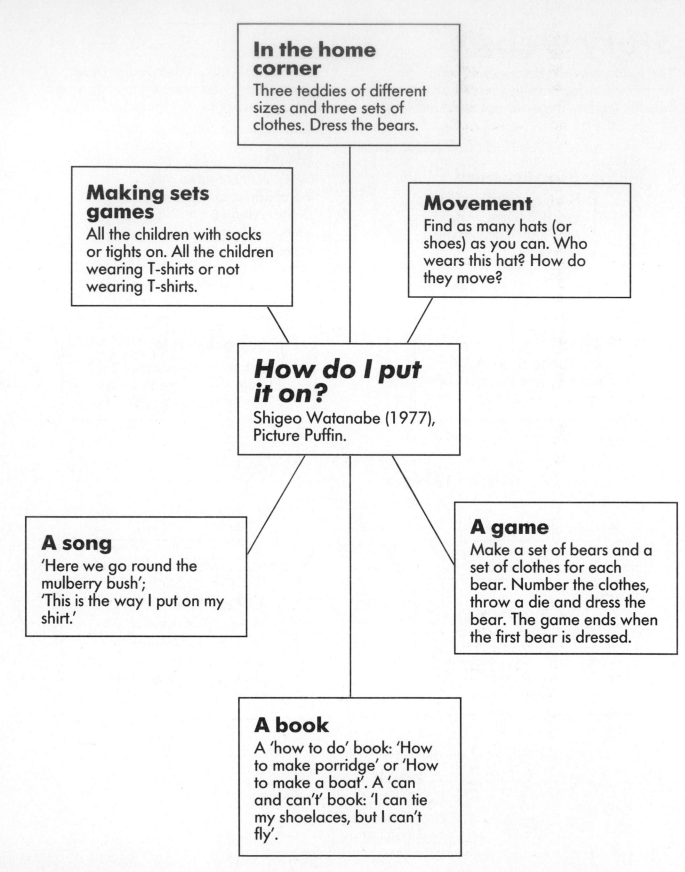

In the home corner
Three teddies of different sizes and three sets of clothes. Dress the bears.

Making sets games
All the children with socks or tights on. All the children wearing T-shirts or not wearing T-shirts.

Movement
Find as many hats (or shoes) as you can. Who wears this hat? How do they move?

How do I put it on?
Shigeo Watanabe (1977), Picture Puffin.

A song
'Here we go round the mulberry bush';
'This is the way I put on my shirt.'

A game
Make a set of bears and a set of clothes for each bear. Number the clothes, throw a die and dress the bear. The game ends when the first bear is dressed.

A book
A 'how to do' book: 'How to make porridge' or 'How to make a boat'. A 'can and can't' book: 'I can tie my shoelaces, but I can't fly'.

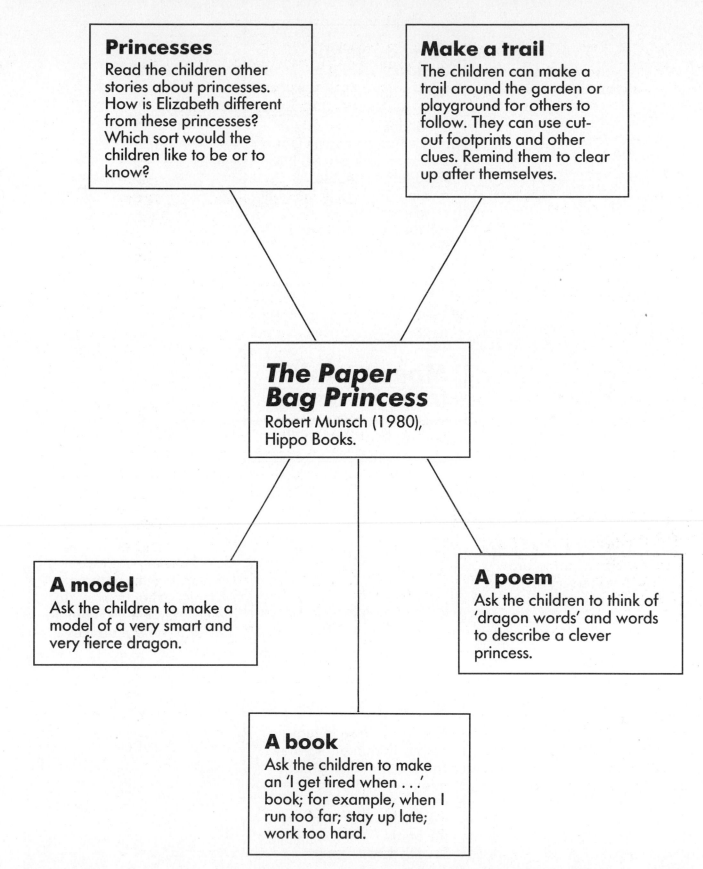

Princesses
Read the children other stories about princesses. How is Elizabeth different from these princesses? Which sort would the children like to be or to know?

Make a trail
The children can make a trail around the garden or playground for others to follow. They can use cut-out footprints and other clues. Remind them to clear up after themselves.

The Paper Bag Princess
Robert Munsch (1980), Hippo Books.

A model
Ask the children to make a model of a very smart and very fierce dragon.

A poem
Ask the children to think of 'dragon words' and words to describe a clever princess.

A book
Ask the children to make an 'I get tired when . . .' book; for example, when I run too far; stay up late; work too hard.

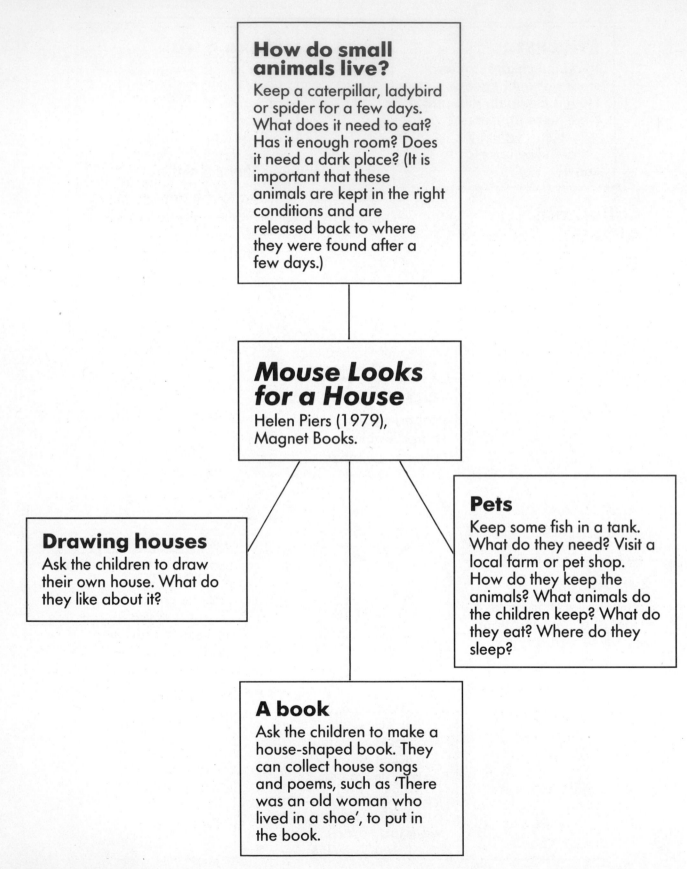

How do small animals live?
Keep a caterpillar, ladybird or spider for a few days. What does it need to eat? Has it enough room? Does it need a dark place? (It is important that these animals are kept in the right conditions and are released back to where they were found after a few days.)

Mouse Looks for a House
Helen Piers (1979), Magnet Books.

Pets
Keep some fish in a tank. What do they need? Visit a local farm or pet shop. How do they keep the animals? What animals do the children keep? What do they eat? Where do they sleep?

Drawing houses
Ask the children to draw their own house. What do they like about it?

A book
Ask the children to make a house-shaped book. They can collect house songs and poems, such as 'There was an old woman who lived in a shoe', to put in the book.

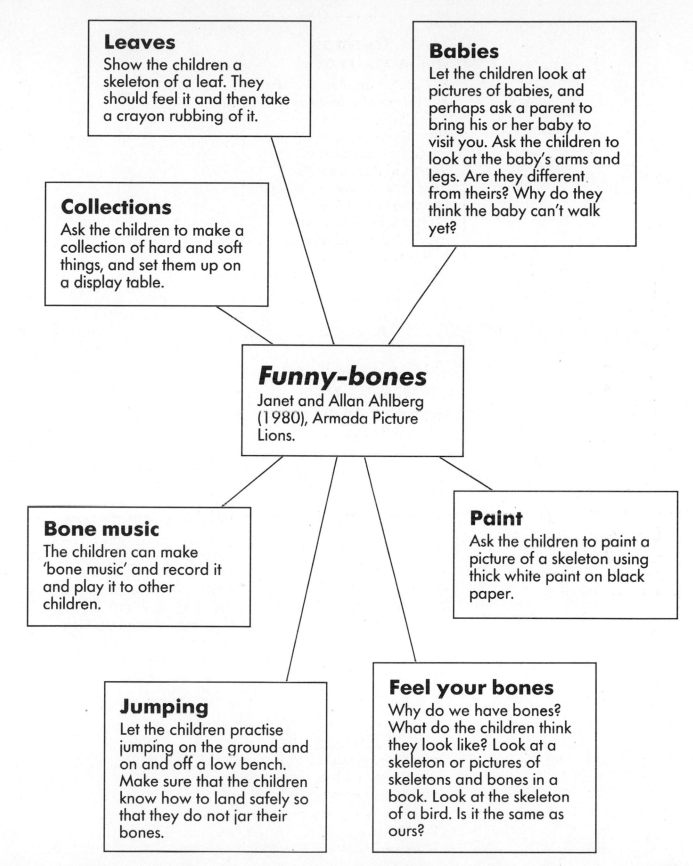

Leaves
Show the children a skeleton of a leaf. They should feel it and then take a crayon rubbing of it.

Babies
Let the children look at pictures of babies, and perhaps ask a parent to bring his or her baby to visit you. Ask the children to look at the baby's arms and legs. Are they different from theirs? Why do they think the baby can't walk yet?

Collections
Ask the children to make a collection of hard and soft things, and set them up on a display table.

Funny-bones
Janet and Allan Ahlberg (1980), Armada Picture Lions.

Bone music
The children can make 'bone music' and record it and play it to other children.

Paint
Ask the children to paint a picture of a skeleton using thick white paint on black paper.

Jumping
Let the children practise jumping on the ground and on and off a low bench. Make sure that the children know how to land safely so that they do not jar their bones.

Feel your bones
Why do we have bones? What do the children think they look like? Look at a skeleton or pictures of skeletons and bones in a book. Look at the skeleton of a bird. Is it the same as ours?

Children's own stories

Chapter three

When children make up and tell their own stories, they use and develop their imagination. They also extend their use of language, which helps them to organise their learning. They learn to order their thoughts in ways that others can follow, and they soon learn about the traditional modes of story-telling. Young children quickly absorb story openings such as 'Once upon a time . . .', 'Once there was . . .' or 'A long time ago . . .' and associate them with the magical experience of story-telling.

Young children can and should be encouraged also to learn to tell the story of more factual happenings, such as a scientific experiment, a cooking episode, or how they built a house with bricks.

Children need a variety of opportunities not only to tell stories, but also to re-create, record and share their stories with others.

Making books together using a variety of formats helps to personalise the text, especially when the subject is a recent experience of a particular child. When the child is familiar with the content she can retell the story most effectively. Modelling texts on children's favourite stories also aids retelling, as it helps to capture the children's interest. Using and extending a range of formats can provide clues as to the meaning and content of the story.

Telling stories

Objective
To encourage and enhance children's ability to tell stories.

What you need
A comfortable area such as the book corner.

What to do
Most children want to tell others their 'news' or share something that has happened to them. This activity provides a way of allowing their enthusiasm to be channelled in a purposeful way.

Ask the children to sit next to a friend, or if that causes too much fuss, to talk to the child sitting next to them. Encourage them to tell each other a story. 'A story' can be defined as something that has happened to them, something that they have heard, or a version of their favourite story. Ensure that one child tells the story while the other one listens, and then reverse the process.

Start this process with only a small number of pairs, so that you can listen to their stories and observe their competence at story-telling. Young children will tell short stories to begin with, but you have to allow for that and help and encourage them to develop the ability to tell longer stories.

Follow-up
When the children can cope with story-telling in twos, ask some of them if they would like to retell the last story they heard to the rest of the group. That way you are encouraging not only their powers of narration but also their listening skills, and their ability to re-create a story in their own words.

Using objects for story-telling

Objective
To develop and encourage powers of narration.

What you need
A variety of objects such as large shells, a piece of material with a hole in it, socks, hats, flowers and so on.

What to do
Choose one of the objects and weave a story around it. You may like to say, for instance, that the material was part of a sail from a boat that sailed around the world. You could tell the children that you were in the boat or your grandmother was a pirate in that ship . . . the possibilities are endless.

Once you have told the story, making sure that it has a beginning, middle and end, you can ask them if they would like to tell their own story about what might have happened or make up their own tales about another object. Very young children will tell short, simple stories and will soon realise how to format a story if provided with good role models.

Follow-up
• When the children have become more practised and competent at telling stories based around an object, you can extend the number of objects to be included in the story.
• Tape the children's stories, and afterwards they can make books or draw pictures to illustrate them.

Making figurines

Objective
To develop the children's language and their recall of events by retelling stories.

What you need
Paper, felt-tipped pens, collage materials, card, scissors, adhesive, a story of your choice.

What to do
Tell or read to the children the story you have chosen. Talk to the children about the different characters, and then let each child make a picture of one of the characters. They should then cut the pictures out, stick them on card and stand them in a menu card holder or small ball of Plasticine. The children can manipulate the figures to retell the story and to make up other stories. When not using the cardboard characters, display them in the listening corner so that the children can play with them.

Follow-up
Help the children to make a backdrop which can be used to make a mini-theatre for retelling stories using the figurines.

Making your own comics

Objective
To help children to sequence their stories.

What you need
Paper, crayons, felt-tipped pens, pencils and other drawing equipment.

What to do
Talk about a favourite story with the children and help them to select four main events from it which they would like to illustrate. Make sure that the events are sequential so that the story will have a beginning, a middle and an end.

Give the children each a piece of paper which has been folded into four sections, with a box drawn around each section. The children should then draw a picture to illustrate one of the incidents in each box. Very young children would probably need to collaborate on this activity, whereas older children should be able to do it on their own.

You can act as a scribe and record the children's words underneath each picture, but encourage the children to write their own speech bubbles and captions as well.

Follow-up
• Make a class or nursery comic by collecting the children's stories together in a big book.
• Let the children make outline pictures for other children to colour in, or make 'dot-to-dot' and 'odd-one-out' puzzles using the same comic-book format.
• Ask the children to use this comic format to record how they made a cake or model.

Zigzag books

Objective
To develop the children's ordering and sequencing abilities by using favourite stories.

What you need
Card or sugar paper, eight smaller pieces of paper for the illustrations, adhesive, felt-tipped pens.

What to do
Choose a well loved story such as 'The three billy goats gruff', 'The old woman and the rice thief', or 'The three little pigs'.

Fold a piece of card in half lengthways; fold it into the middle, and then fold it back on itself to produce eight faces (see illustration).

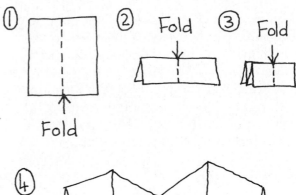

Ask the children to retell the story and act as scribe to record the story in the children's words in the zigzag book. You should decide between you what illustrations are needed and who will draw them.

Follow-up

● Use zigzag books to record the children's versions of an outing.
● Make zigzag number books with ten pages showing the numbers up to ten.

Photo books

Objectives

To use photographs as a way of involving children in stories, and to give them opportunities to retell and reread their stories with friends.

What you need

A simple camera.

What to do

Ask the children to take photographs of each other or help you to do so. If the children are taking the photographs themselves a useful tip is to tell them to hold their breath and squeeze their elbows into their sides while they take it. This will often help to reduce the amount of camera shake, but you must be prepared to use photographs that are neither in focus nor beautifully composed!

Together, choose a favourite story, for example, 'The enormous turnip' and retell the story using the photographs of the children instead of the characters in the story – 'Ayesha pulled and pulled but she could not pull up the enormous turnip'.

The photographs can then be stuck into a book together with some simple captions, and left in the book corner so that the children can retell the story to each other.

Follow-up

● Have another set of photographs printed and put them in a zigzag book (see page 72) or a pop-up book (see page 77). The children can take it in turns to take the books home to share them with their families.
● Let the children choose their own stories and use their friends as characters.

Alphabet books

Objective
To reinforce the children's knowledge of the alphabet.

What you need
Large pieces of card, smaller pieces of paper, felt-tipped pens, adhesive.

What to do
Make a zigzag book with twenty-six pages in it (see Zigzag books, page 72). Ask the children to choose a letter that they are familiar with (perhaps the first letter of their name). Try to ensure that you have as many different letters of the alphabet as possible. Then ask the children either to draw or to collage their particular letter. Together with the children stick the letters into the zigzag book in sequence and display them so that the children can see the alphabet. Any letters not chosen by the children can be supplied by adult helpers.

Follow-up
Suggest that the children make letters from construction models, their own body shapes, dough or clay. Photograph the letter shapes. Make these photographs into another alphabet zigzag book.

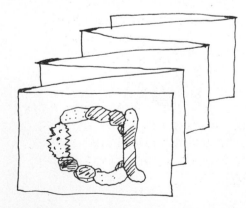

Make a felt board

Objective
To make an aid to support story-telling.

What you need
Two large pieces of stiff card, felt, thick white adhesive, linson (book-binding tape) or carpet tape about 15cm wide, paper or fabric, two large hooks and eyes.

What to do
Spread the thick white adhesive evenly over one of the large pieces of card. It helps if you begin from the middle and work outwards radially, as this ensures a more even coating of adhesive. Next carefully lay the felt on to the card, using the flat of your hand to remove any air bubbles and creases, while trying to avoid stretching the felt. Make sure that there is enough felt left around the edges of the card to fold over, as if you were wrapping a parcel. Cover the other piece of board or thick card in the same way and leave them to dry under something heavy like a book, or use a book press if you have access to one, otherwise the boards will buckle.

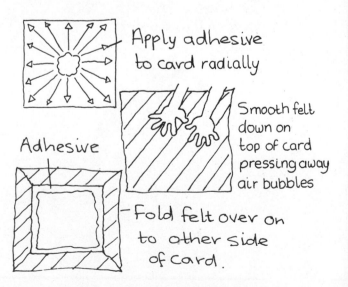

Apply adhesive to card radially

Smooth felt down on top of card pressing away air bubbles

Adhesive

Fold felt over on to other side of card.

Use the carpet tape or spread the linson with adhesive and place the boards on to it felt side down, side by side but leaving a small gap between them to make a hinge. Fold the excess tape underneath and the two boards will be joined together. Then stick the paper or material on the insides of the two boards to make a neat finish and hide all the joins. Press the board again while it dries.

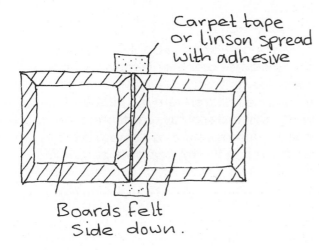

Carpet tape or linson spread with adhesive

Boards felt side down.

Finally, attach the large hooks and eyes by sticking them with strong adhesive to the top and bottom of the board. The board will be able to stand on its own and thus be used by two children listening to different stories.

Hook and eye fastened in place.

Story board figures

Objective
To give children concrete support for telling and retelling stories with the aid of a felt or magnetic story board.

What you need
Lengths of Velcro, magnetic tape, thin card, paper, felt-tipped pens, clear self-adhesive plastic covering.

What to do
Depending upon your ability as an illustrator, either draw or trace the characters from a favourite children's picture book. Cut them out and cover them in self-adhesive plastic covering to make them more durable. Cut and stick on to the cut-outs small pieces of either Velcro (for use with a felt board, see page 72) or magnetic tape (for use with a magnet board). If you are using Velcro you will only need to use the piece with the 'claws', which will easily attach itself to the felt.

Once the figures have been completed you can tell a story to the children using the figures as support props. You should leave the figures by the felt board once you have finished so that the children can tell each other stories in their own time.

Follow-up
• Build up a stock of characters from different stories. Store them in easily recognisable folders or clear plastic wallets.
• Tape readings of the stories to go with the characters and leave them in the listening corner (see page 20) together with the board and figures. The children can then move the figures as they listen to the story.

Changing the ending of a story

Objective
To allow children to explore the concept of 'What if . . .'.

What you need
A well-known and favourite story, blank books.

What to do
When you have told the story, ask the children to take part in a game of 'What if . . .'. For example what if the Gingerbread Boy had said no to the fox's invitation to cross the river?

Share different children's ideas and reactions orally at first, and then help the children to record their ideas into books. You will need to scribe for very young children, but allow children to write for themselves if they are able.

Books with flaps

Objective
To promote discussion and use of language of position using *Where's Spot?* by Eric Hill as a model.

What you need
Folded card, scissors, masking tape, paper or an exercise book, pencils or felt-tipped pens, a camera.

What to do
Photograph the children as they work in different areas of the nursery or school;

for instance, playing in the garden, washing in the cloakroom, reading in the book corner and so on. Use the text of *Where's Spot?* as a model, and write some suitable text on one page of the book, for example: 'Where is Rita? Is she in the garden?' Then stick the photograph of Rita playing in the garden on the facing page and cover it with a piece of card. Use masking tape to make a hinge so that the card can be lifted by the children to find out where Rita is.

Follow-up
• Make a number of books in this way, hiding either objects or number symbols under the flaps.
• Ask the children to play 'hide and seek', hiding a soft toy. Encourage them to ask questions such as 'Where is the teddy? Is it in the toy cupboard?'

Pop-up books

Objective

To make a book that will stimulate children's story-telling.

What you need

Large sheets of sugar paper, scissors, felt-tipped pens.

What to do

Ask the children to fold a sheet of sugar paper into four and press the creases firmly. They should then unfold the paper and refold it in half lengthways. Next, they can cut a small slit at right angles to the long fold about two thirds of the way down the lower half. They should unfold the paper again and refold it into four. The slit will now be inside the book. The children should ease their fingers under the slit and gently pull out the top and bottom of it to make a 'mouth'. Then they should close the book and press the creases firmly.

Ask the children to draw a face around the mouth and then to tell a story about the character.

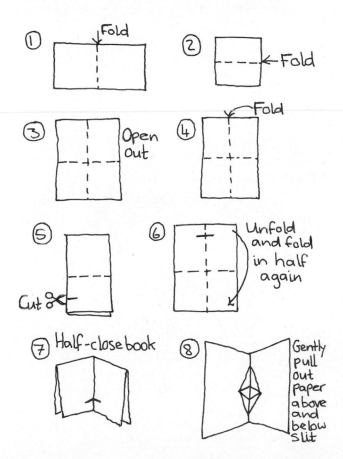

Photo recall

Objectives

To recall an experience and promote discussion.

What you need

A simple camera.

What to do

Together with a small group of children, make a trip to the local shops. Take photographs of events during the trip, such as leaving school, arriving at the shop, choosing an item from the shelf, paying for the item and so on. Try not to take too many photographs; four to six is enough.

When you return to the nursery or classroom use the photographs with the children to recall the trip. Put the pictures in sequence and encourage the children to use them to help tell what happened.

Follow-up

● Encourage the children to use the photographs to tell others about the trip.
● Make a zigzag book with the photographs but without text (see page 72).

Group stories

Objective
To encourage children to develop a story.

What you need
A comfortable area.

What to do
Sit in a circle on the floor with a small group of children. Start by telling them a short story, but stop before you reach a conclusion. Ask the child sitting on your right if she can continue the story. When you think that she has said enough, make a pre-arranged noise (you might jangle your keys, for instance) and tell the next child on the right to continue telling the story. Carry on around the circle until all the children have had a go, and bring the story to a conclusion yourself.

Initially you must be prepared for short stories, but as children become more experienced, you will find that their stories become longer and more confident. When this happens you can enlarge the size of the group.

Follow-up
Encourage different children to begin a story and end one. Let the children take turns to make whatever noise has been agreed as the signal to stop.

Shared reading

Chapter four

Shared reading has many strengths when used in the classroom. It offers opportunities and experiences for children to see the whole reading process 'in action'. As well as being a good way of sharing a story, shared reading also introduces children to the features of texts, including letters, words and punctuation, within a meaningful context.

Shared reading encourages children to work together and to share meanings and ideas. It allows them to join in at their own level, from the very earliest stages of understanding how books work.

Through shared reading, children become familiar with story, and gradually become able to read the texts for themselves. It has tremendous advantages for bilingual children and supports children learning a second language because the process encourages collaboration. The texts can be shared between children, between children and adults, in small groups or with the whole class; there are no hard and fast rules.

When used regularly, as part of the children's literacy development, shared reading helps children to build up a knowledge of books and to develop their own favourites. Eventually they begin to know stories well enough to 'read' for themselves and make very close approximations to the text.

Shared reading is not only important for language and literacy development, but forms part of a wider theory of learning. It is by nature collaborative, and allows children and teachers to work together on something that would be impossible if attempted on an individual basis.

There is also scope for sharing books other than stories, for example poetry, songs and traditional nursery rhymes. Writing can also be shared, from letters to records of an outing or a cooking event; the scope is endless.

Making big books

Objective
To make a resource that children can read and share together.

What you need
Large sheets of white sugar paper, a large sheet of coloured card, thick felt-tipped pens, crayons.

What to do
Before you start collaborating on a big book you need to choose a favourite story. Ask the children to retell the story in their own words, making notes of what they say. Discuss the illustrations that you will need, and let the children decide who will illustrate which part of the story. The children can work together on an illustration, but you do need to organise and make sure that they are not all illustrating the same section. Then, together, decide where the pictures and the writing will go. Initially you may find you have to give children support, but they will soon become extremely competent and will enjoy the process.

When the final format has been decided, stick the pictures into a book made from large pieces of sugar paper, and write or word process the text. Talk with the children about your writing and ask them informally about their own knowledge of writing in general. For example, do they recognise any letters from their name?

Attach a cover (which should be made from fairly stiff coloured card) to the finished text, and write the title and the authors' and illustrators' names on the front. Staple or sew the whole book together.

Follow-up
- Photocopy and reduce the big book

and make a set of small books for the children to read together. The large book will continue to be an invaluable reading source which you can use with a group of children.

• Try to build up a stock of enlarged texts. Use rhymes, songs and the children's favourite stories to enhance their awareness of print and to develop their understanding of story.

Using pictures instead of words

Objective

To make a resource to use in a group situation to help children to focus on the individual words in a text.

What you need

Big sheets of paper, an easel, two large sheets of white sugar paper folded in half, small pieces of paper about 5cm × 2.5cm, pencils, crayons.

What to do

Working with a group of about six children, ask them to retell one of their favourite stories together. Write down their words on the large sheets of paper which should be attached to the easel. When the children have finished you can read the text and edit it together. Once you have all agreed on the final written format, write the text on the sugar paper in big writing, leaving spaces instead of writing the names of objects. Ask the children to draw pictures of the missing objects on the small pieces of paper and stick them in the spaces.

When you have finished making the book you can use it as a 'reading together' book. Prop it up on the easel or on a chair where it can be seen by all the children, and read the text to the children while they join in by 'reading' the pictures.

Follow-up

• Write out the missing words on small pieces of paper or card. Can the children find where the words should go?

• Make another big book with the same text. Do not leave out any words this time, but ask the children to draw pictures of the objects on small pieces of paper. These can then be stuck on a flap of card above the corresponding words in the text. The children can lift the flap to match the word to the picture.

Paired reading

Objectives
To give older readers regular reading practice and to provide support for the younger reader.

What you need
Older readers, maybe upper infants or junior age children.

What to do
You need to negotiate with teachers of an older class of children so that you can carry out this activity. It works well where some of the older children are less competent readers for their age, because it gives the older child the 'status' of reading to another child while at the same time supporting the older child's reading.

It is important to fix a regular time each week when the children can read together, possibly sharing classrooms, taking turns and so on. If the whole class is involved it puts less pressure on the less competent readers.

The older children should read with a younger child, choosing mainly books found in the nursery or reception class. Encourage the children to share and discuss their favourite books together, as this not only supports the older child's reading, but also develops the younger child's knowledge of stories.

Follow-up
Try changing or rotating the classes involved every term. The children should try to build up their own 'tried and tested' reviews of some of their most enjoyable books, with the younger children participating in the composing, writing and illustrating as much as possible.

Taking books home

Objective
To help families to enjoy books together.

What you need
A folder for each child, an exercise book.

What to do
Let the children decorate their folders so that they are able to recognise their own.

Set aside the last 20 minutes of one day each week so that the children can select a book to take home with them. If possible, carers can help their children to choose books, but you need to have sufficient space for this to be done comfortably. Alternatively (and this is often possible in a nursery), carers can come in to select a book with their child at any time of the day.

Carers should record the name of their child and the book they have selected in the exercise book which should be kept in the book corner. Make sure that these are always filled in. In each child's folder put a card or small book on which the carer can write any comments about the child's reaction to a book. The child can keep in the folder any drawings or written work inspired by a book.

A very big turnip book

Objective
To make a big book which children can read together.

What you need
A large sheet of white sugar paper or card folded in half, drawing paper, pencils, crayons, magazines, adhesive, an easel, *The Great Big Enormous Turnip* by Alexei Tolstoy and Helen Oxenbury.

What to do
After reading *The Great Big Enormous Turnip* ask one or two children to look at the turnip and draw a large one on the sugar paper or card. They should try to make it as big as they can.

Cut the picture out, being very careful to leave some spare paper to act as the spine of the book. You should use this shape as a template and cut out a number of folded sheets of paper to make pages.

Fix the book together either by stapling along the fold with a long-arm stapler or by sewing the folded edge. Attach the cover by stapling it on the uncut edge to the front of the book. Let the children select pictures of different types of vegetables and stick them in the book. Alternatively, ask them to make collage pictures by sticking in scraps of torn paper from magazines.

Put the book on an easel or a chair where all the children can see it. Use it as part of a vegetable or food project to promote discussion. What are the children's favourite vegetables? Which vegetables don't they like? Why do they think they should eat lots of vegetables?

Follow-up
• Make a set of individual small turnip books.
• Try printing with turnips.
• Cook with turnips. Try making turnip soup.

'My name is . . .'

Objective
To make a set of books that become a reading-together resource.

What you need
A big book made from a folded sheet of card about 76cm wide and 20cm deep, cards for all the children about 20cm long and 5cm deep, a thick felt-tipped pen, sticky tape, scissors.

What to do
Using a thick felt-tipped pen write 'My name is . . .' on the left-hand side of the card book. On the right-hand side, at the same level, cut two vertical slits about 15cm apart and just over 5cm deep. Strengthen the slits by placing a piece of sticky tape on each side of the card where the slits are, and cutting through the tape. Once you have finished making the book you should prop it up on an

easel or chair, where a group of children can see it. Then you can slot different name cards between the slits to complete the sentence; for example 'My name is Helen'. Can the children read their own names? Can they read their friend's name?

A word matching book

Objectives

To focus children's attention on the individual words that make sentences, and to provide a resource which can be taken home and shared with parents and family.

What you need

Paper folded in half to make a book, felt-tipped pens, pencils, small pieces of card, envelope, adhesive.

What to do

Fold up the bottom edge of the book about 2.5cm and staple the sides, leaving the top open to form a wallet. Ask the children to draw a picture on the top half of the book above the wallet and to dictate to you one sentence. Write this sentence on the folded section.

Write each word from the sentence on individual pieces of card, leaving 2.5cm

below the writing. The children can then take the word cards and match them up with the words in the sentence. They should slot each word into the wallet so that the word shows above. Ask the children to work with a friend and match each other's sentences. The owner of the book should then read the sentence back to his or her friend.

Stick an envelope on the back of the book and keep the word cards inside it so that they don't get lost. Let the children take the books home and read them with their family or carers.

Parents and teachers working together

Chapter five

Before children come to nursery or start school they have learned a wide variety of skills. They have seen a lot and done a lot and are busy processing a great deal of information.

Parents and carers are the first educators and have the best and most detailed information about their children. Therefore, there are educational gains to be made for children when their carers and teachers work together.

Inviting parents to come and work with you in the nursery or classroom takes some care and preparation. So often parents are invited only to find themselves confined to washing paint pots or helping with the sewing.

In this chapter we make some suggestions about ways to involve parents in your class or nursery, and make use of their skills, understanding and knowledge. By joining in, parents and carers can gain some understanding of the methods and aims of the nursery or school.

The history of the locality

Objective
To introduce historical concepts through hearing local people's stories of their childhood.

What you need
A parent, carer or grandparent who lived in the area as a child, photographs from their childhood if possible, old money or other mementoes.

What to do
Invite a local parent or carer to come into the school or nursery to talk to the children. Speak to her beforehand and try to decide on a theme for the talk. Choose something that the children already have some knowledge of, such as getting lost, the first day at school, going shopping or games they used to play.

Make sure that the speaker is sitting comfortably and ask her to talk to a small group of children as if she were talking to her own children. Afterwards the children can talk to the speaker about her experiences, asking any questions they may have and thinking about their own experiences; do the same sorts of thing happen nowadays? What is different? Do they know any of the places that the speaker talked about?

Follow-up

• Take the children out to visit some of the places the speaker mentioned.
• The children can write down or draw pictures of the speaker's reminiscences, which can be made into a book and left in the book corner.

History of other places

Objectives

To help the children to begin to understand that people move around the country and from country to country, and that children growing up in different times and places still have a lot in common.

What you need

A parent, carer or grandparent who will come in and talk about their life as a child in another town or country.

What to do

Ask a parent or carer who was brought up in another area or country to come in and tell the children about their childhood experiences. They could use the same themes as the local speaker in the previous activity.

The same discussion process can take place once the speaker has finished.

Follow-up

• Ask the children to gather a collection of photographs of their parents and carers when they were children — these are often precious so put them in plastic wallets if the children are to handle them. Do they look the same as their children do now? Can the children find any differences in clothes, hairstyles and so on?
• Make a display of photographs showing all the adults in the school or nursery when they were babies. Can the children recognise who they are?

Have a story day

Objectives

To show children how much we value stories, and to involve parents and other members of the community.

What you need

A group of parents or friends who will work with you, people who will visit and tell the children stories, tea and coffee, cakes and biscuits.

What to do

Let everyone know well in advance that you are going to have a story day. The children can write or draw invitations to be sent to local people to ask them to come and tell stories for the story day. Find out in advance what stories the story-tellers will tell, and try to ensure that you have a balance of different types, including traditional, modern and true stories, and ones from different countries.

On the day, organise the children into small groups to listen to the stories. They can then move from story-teller to story-teller in these groups listening to the stories. Make sure that each group hears at least three or four stories in the day.

Finish the day by serving tea to all the contributors. Alternatively, the staff can put on a play for the children; a pantomime based on a traditional story can be put together fairly quickly and takes very little skill!

Have a story week

Objective
To immerse children in stories and story-telling for a week.

What you need
Adult helpers.

What to do
Before story week begins, try to fill the school or nursery with pictures, posters and story books.

Arrange for people to come into the school or nursery and tell stories at least twice a day. You could also try out some of the following activities:
● Ask a story-teller to come and tell stories to the children. Invite parents as well. A local library will often send someone to read stories, or you may have a good story-teller among your staff or the parents.
● Hire a puppet theatre company.
● Invite a children's author to come and talk about his or her work to the children. If one lives locally so much the better, but if not, try contacting the publisher of books you and the children like.

● Invite a book illustrator to visit the children to talk about his or her work. Again, publishers will advise you how to contact a suitable person.
● Contact a publisher and find out whether they would be prepared to set up a book display in your school or nursery.
● Cook porridge and hold a 'Three bears party' (providing other treats as well as porridge!) or have a 'Mr Gumpy tea party' or a 'teddy bears' picnic'. Invite the children's families and younger sisters and brothers to come along.
● Ask the children to draw pictures of scenes or characters from the books they like and send them to the authors.
● Visit the local children's library or arrange for a visit from the librarian.
● Ask a parent with a video-camera to record some of the events so that the film can be shown at staff meetings and parents' evenings.

Parents as translators

Objective
To enlist parents' help to provide texts in different languages.

What you need
Simple attractive books that are popular in your class.

What to do
Ask parents, older sisters or brothers or other people who speak and write the children's home languages to write their version of one of the children's favourite books in this language. They should write it on strips of paper which can be pasted above the English text. These books can be displayed so that the children can compare the languages or scripts.

Ask parents to read the books out loud so that children who do not speak these languages can hear how they sound.

Making a school bookshop

Objectives
To enable children to save up to buy a book and to provide a chance for children and carers to select books together.

What you need
A group of people who are willing to spend a couple of hours a week organising and administrating a bookshop, a place to lay out the books and a safe place to keep them, an account book, contact with a good local bookshop or book club; children's savings cards.

What to do
Speak to your local bookshop before setting up a school shop; they may be able to let you have a discount on the books. Bookshops will often allow a school to have a selection of books and delay the payment until the books are sold.

Hold the bookshop regularly (half an hour before going home time works well). Select three or four children to work with the organisers each week, helping to set the shop up and so on. Try to make sure that the books are laid out attractively. The children will learn to handle books properly as they become more experienced at helping, and they should be encouraged to recommend their own favourites to other children.

One member of staff can collect the money from the children who want to save up for a book, and should enter the amount on each child's card. Children will often decide to save their money instead of spending it on sweets or crisps if they have a special book in mind. Be sure to write it down immediately and let them see that you have entered it on their record card.

Follow-up
Hopefully a small profit will be made from running a bookshop and the children can help you decide how it should be spent.

A parents' workshop

Objective
To help parents understand how they can help with children's reading.

What you need
A suitable place for the meeting, tea, coffee, biscuits.

What to do
Have this meeting when you are planning a scheme to allow the children to take books home or organising a story day, or simply use it to discuss the

school's reading policy. Plan it at a time when most of the parents can attend. You may need to hold more than one and at different times of the day.

Have the meeting in a comfortable place and set out the chairs in a circle to create an informal atmosphere. Try to provide tea or coffee and biscuits.

Explain why you think it is useful for children to read at home with their families. Try to put across the pleasure that books and stories can bring children and the fact that they will be learning as they read. Talk about the need for both child and parents to feel relaxed and comfortable so that they can easily look at the book together and take the time to enjoy the story. Parents should not expect their children to recognise all the words,

but talking about the pictures may help them to discover what the words say. Also tell them that they need only put aside a short period of time each day to read with their children.

Explain that it is useful for the teacher if parents record the child's reaction to a book; did the child enjoy it? Did he join in with the story-telling? Does he know the story?

Follow-up

After talking to the parents and finding out their questions and difficulties, produce a small, simply-written and clear leaflet that can be photocopied and given to the parents to remind them of what was said at the meeting and to help those who didn't come.

Bibliography

Children's books

Ahlberg, A. and Ahlberg, J. (1978), *Each Peach Pear Plum*, Viking Kestrel/Picture Puffin.

Ahlberg, A. and Ahlberg, J. (1980), *Mrs Wobble the Waitress*, Viking Kestrel/Young Puffin.

Ahlberg, A. and McNaughton, C. (1981), *Miss Brick the Builder's Baby*, Viking Kestrel/Young Puffin.

Ahlberg, A. and Wright, J. (1980), *Mrs Plug the Plumber*, Viking Kestrel/Young Puffin.

Ahlberg, J. and Ahlberg, A. (1984), *The Baby's Catalogue*, Viking Kestrel/Picture Puffin.

Ahlberg, J. and Ahlberg, A. (1980), *Funny-bones*, Heinemann/Armada Picture Lions.

Ahlberg, J. and Ahlberg, A. (1986), *The Jolly Postman*, Heinemann.

Ahlberg, J. and Ahlberg, A. (1983), *Peepo!*, Viking Kestrel/Picture Puffin.

Armitage, R. and Armitage, D. (1977), *The Lighthouse Keeper's Lunch*, Deutsch/Picture Puffin.

Bang, M. (1983), *Ten, Nine, Eight*, Julia MacRae Books/Picture Puffin.

Baum, L. and Bouma, P. (1986), *Are we nearly there?*, Bodley Head/Magnet.

Baum, L. and Daly, N. (1984), *I Want to See the Moon*, Bodley Head/Magnet.

Berenstain, S. and Berenstain, J. (1972), *Bears in the Night*, Collins.

Berenstain, S. and Berenstain, J. (1979), *The Berenstain Bears and the Spooky Old Tree*, Collins.

Berenstain, S. and Berenstain, J. (1974), *He Bear She Bear*, Collins.

Berry, J. (1987), *A Thief in the Village and Other Stories*, Hamish Hamilton.

Blake, Q. (1980), *Mr Magnolia*, Cape/Armada Picture Lions.

Bradman, T. and Browne, E. (1988), *Through My Window*, Little Mammoth.

Bradman, T. and Browne, E. (1988), *Wait and See*, Little Mammoth.

Breinburg, P. (1978), *My Brother Sean*, Picture Puffin.

Briggs, R. (1978), *The Snowman*, Hamish Hamilton/Picture Puffin.

Browne, A. (1988), *The Little Bear Book*, Hamish Hamilton/Macmillan.

Burningham, J. (1988), *Grandpa*, Cape/Picture Puffin.

Burningham, J. (1978), *Mr Gumpy's Outing*, Cape/Picture Puffin.

Burningham, J. (1980), *The Shopping Basket*, Cape/Armada Picture Lions.

Burningham, J. (1985), *Time to Get Out of the Bath, Shirley*, Cape/Armada Picture Lions.

Burningham, J. (1978), *Would You Rather . . .*, Cape/Armada Picture Lions.

Campbell, R. (1987), *Dear Zoo*, Campbell Blackie/Picture Puffin.

Campbell, R. (1988), *My Presents*, Campbell Books.

Carle, E. (1971), *Do You Want to Be My Friend?*, Picture Puffin.

Carle, E. (1988), *The Very Busy Spider*, Hamish Hamilton.

Carle, E. (1971), *The Very Hungry Caterpillar*, Hamish Hamilton/Picture Puffin.

Counsel, J. (1986), *But Martin!*, Picture Corgi.

Cutler, I. (1980), *Meal One*, Heinemann/Armada Picture Lions.

Daly, N. (1986), *Look at Me!*, Walker Books.

Edwards, H. and Niland, D. (1980), *There's a Hippopotamus on Our Roof Eating Cake*, Picture Knight.

Flournoy, V. (1985), *The Patchwork Quilt*, Bodley Head/Picture Puffin.

Foreman, M. (1982), *The Land of Dreams*, Andersen Press.

Garland, S. (1985), *Going Shopping*, Picture Puffin.

Hawkins, C. and Hawkins, J. (1987), *Here's a Happy Elephant*, Walker Books.

Hawkins, C. and Hawkins, J. (1984), *Mig the Pig*, Piccadilly Press/Picture Puffin.

Hawkins, C. (1987), *Mr Wolf's Week*, Armada Picture Lions.

Hawkins, C. (1983), *What's the Time, Mr Wolf?*, Heinemann/Armada Picture Lions.

Hill, E. (1981), *Spot's First Walk*, Heinemann/Picture Puffin.

Hill, E. (1980), *Where's Spot?*, Heinemann/Picture Puffin.

Hughes, S. (1981), *Alfie Gets In First*, Bodley Head/Armada Picture Lions.

Hughes, S. (1982), *Alfie's Feet*, Bodley Head/Armada Picture Lions.

Hutchins, P. (1971), *Changes, Changes*, Bodley Head.

Hutchins, P. (1974), *Clocks and More Clocks*, Picture Puffin.

Hutchins, P. (1976), *Don't Forget the Bacon!*, Bodley Head/Picture Puffin.

Hutchins, P. (1986), *The Doorbell Rang*, Bodley Head/Picture Puffin.

Hutchins, P. (1973), *Goodnight Owl!*, Bodley Head/Picture Puffin.

Hutchins, P. (1978), *Happy Birthday, Sam*, Bodley Head/Picture Puffin.

Hutchins, P. (1968), *Rosie's Walk*, Bodley Head/Picture Puffin.

Hutchins, P. (1972), *Titch*, Bodley Head/Picture Puffin.

Hutchins, P. (1983), *You'll Soon Grow Into Them, Titch*, Bodley Head/Picture Puffin.

Lloyd, E. (1978), *Nandy's Bedtime*, Bodley Head.

Lloyd, E. (1978), *Nini at Carnival*, Bodley Head/Picture Puffin.

Mahy, M. (1975), *The Boy Who Was Followed Home*, Little Mammoth.

Mahy, M. (1985), *Jam*, Little Mammoth.

Mahy, M. (1985), *The Man Whose Mother was a Pirate*, Picture Puffin.

Maris, R. (1986), *Are You There Bear?*, Picture Puffin.

McKee, D. (1980), *Not Now, Bernard*, Andersen Press/Arrow.

McKee, D. (1988), *Who's a Clever Baby Then?*, Andersen Press.

Munsch, R. (1980), *The Paper Bag Princess*, Hippo Books.

Murphy, J. (1986), *Five Minutes' Peace*, Walker Books.

Murphy, J. (1982), *Peace at Last*, Macmillan Picturemac.

Murphy, J. (1989), *A Piece of Cake*, Walker Books.

Murphy, J. (1983), *Whatever Next?*, Walker Books.

Oram, H. (1982), *Angry Arthur*, Andersen Press.

Ormerod, J. (1983), *Moonlight*, Picture Puffin.

Ormerod, J. (1983), *Sunshine*, Picture Puffin.

Oxenbury, H. (1985), *I Can*, Sainsbury's/Walker Books.

Oxenbury, H. (1984), *Our Dog*, Walker Books.

Oxenbury, H. (1988), *Tom and Pippo Read a Story*, Walker Books.

Patel, M. (1974), *Rupa the Elephant*, National Book Trust, India.

Piers, H. (1979), *Mouse Looks for a House*, Magnet Books.

Prater, J. (1985), *The Gift*, Bodley Head/Picture Puffin.

Rice, E. (1983), *Good-night, Good-night*, Picture Puffin.

Sendak, M. (1967), *Where the Wild Things Are*, Bodley Head/Picture Puffin.

Simeon, L. (1984), *Marcellus*, Akira Press.

Singh, R. (1988), *The Indian Story Book*, Heinemann.

Sutton, E. and Dodd, L. (1978), *My Cat Likes to Hide in Boxes*, Picture Puffin.

Swindells, R. (1981), *Norah and the Whale*, Wheaton.

Thomas, I. (1986), *Janine and the New Baby*, Deutsch/Little Mammoth.

Tolstoy, A. and Oxenbury, H. (1988), *The Great Big Enormous Turnip*, Armada Picture Lions.

Vipont, E. and Briggs, R. (1969), *The Elephant and the Bad Baby*, Hamish Hamilton/Picture Puffin.

Watanabe, S. (1977), *How Do I Put it On?*, Picture Puffin.

Watanabe, S. (1985), *I Can Build a House!*, Picture Puffin.

Watanabe, S. (1984), *I Can Do It*, Picture Puffin.

Wildsmith, B. (1983), *All Fall Down*, Oxford University Press.

Wildsmith, B. (1982), *Cat on the Mat*, Oxford University Press.

Wilkes, A. (1990), *My First Nature Book*, Dorling Kindersley.

Wilkes, A. (1990), *My First Science Book*, Dorling Kindersley.

Poetry books

Agard, J. (1983), *I Din Do Nuttin*, Bodley Head.

Agard, J. (1986), *Say It Again, Granny*, Bodley Head.

Bayley, N. (1976), *Book of Nursery Rhymes*, Cape/Picture Puffin.

Foster, J. L. (1985), *A Very First Poetry Book*, Oxford University Press.

Mann, R. and Mann, A. (1980), *Mother Goose Comes to Cable Street*, Picture Puffin.

Milligan, S. (1971), *Book of Milliganimals*, Puffin.

Milligan, S. (1970), *Silly Verse for Kids*, Puffin.

Nichols, G. (1988), *Come On Into My Tropical Garden*, A & C Black.

Nicoll, H. (Ed) (1984), *Poems for 7 Year Olds and Under*, Puffin.

Opie, I. and Opie, P. (1970), *Puffin Book of Nursery Rhymes*, Puffin.

Further reading for teachers and parents

Centre for Language in Primary Education (1990), *Shared Reading, Shared Writing*, CLPE.

Hester, H. (1983), *Stories in the Multilingual Primary Classroom*, Harcourt Brace Jovanovich.

Meek, M. (1987), *How Texts Teach What Readers Learn*, Thimble Press.

Meek, M. (1990), *On Being Literate*, Bodley Head.

Meek, M. (Ed), (1983), *Opening Moves*, Bedford Way Papers No. 17, University of London, Institute of Education.

Meek, M. (1985), 'Play and Paradoxes: Some Considerations of Imagination and Language' in Wells, G. and Nicholls, J. (Eds) *Language and Learning: An Interactional Perspective*, The Falmer Press.

Meek, M. (1981) *Reading*, Bodley Head.

Meek, M. and Mills, C. (Eds) (1988), *Language and Literacy in the Primary School*, The Falmer Press.

Smith, F. (1978), *Reading*, Cambridge University Press.

Waterland, L. (1985), *Read With Me*, Thimble Press.

Whitehead, M. R. (1991), *Language and Literacy in the Early Years*, Paul Chapman.